The Wild West in England

D0110874

THE PAPERS OF WILLIAM F. "BUFFALO BILL" CODY

WILLIAM F. CODY

The Wild West in England

Edited and with an introduction by Frank Christianson

University of Nebraska Press
Lincoln & London

East Baton Rouge Parish Library
Baton Rouge, Louisiana

© 2012 by the Board of Regents of the
University of Nebraska. All rights reserved
Manufactured in the United States of America

Support for this volume was provided by the State of Wyoming

Library of Congress Cataloging-in-Publication Data
Buffalo Bill, 1846–1917.
The Wild West in England / William F. Cody; edited and
with an introduction by Frank Christianson.
p. cm. — (The papers of William F. "Buffalo Bill" Cody)
Includes bibliographical references and index.
ISBN 978-0-8032-4388-0 (cloth: alk. paper) —
ISBN 978-0-8032-4054-4 (pbk.: alk. paper)
1. Buffalo Bill's Wild West Show—History.
2. Wild west shows—England—History.
3. Buffalo Bill, 1846–1917—Travel—England.
4. Pioneers—West (U.S.)—Biography.
5. Entertainers—United States—Biography.
I. Christianson, Frank. II. Title.
GV1821.B8A3 2012
791.8'4—dc23
2012014820

Set in Iowan Old Style by Bob Reitz.

CONTENTS

ILLUSTRATIONS

SERIES EDITOR'S PREFACE

The central question facing the McCracken Research Library six years ago when it launched The Papers of William F. "Buffalo Bill" Cody was basic: why should Cody's papers be edited and published? Cody was not a great statesman; he was not an important philosopher nor a literary genius. Though widely recognized as a show business pioneer, his contribution to cultural consciousness and advancement has too often been, and in large measure continues to be, relegated to the margins of American history. Cody is readily accepted as a pop culture icon of his day but not always seen as a subject of serious scholarly study.

As this present volume illustrates, William Cody deserves the level of attention afforded by this documentary editing project not because of his intellectual, economic, or political contribution but, rather, in part, because he was the most successful cultural export in American history. No other enterprise before or since has so boldly claimed to represent the American experience. Moreover, Cody did not merely represent American culture—he defined it for generations of Europeans. In so doing, he gave it a definition that resonates today. From Cody's prescient perspective, the United States is a pluralist, multicultural, exceptional nation. For European audiences, Buffalo Bill's Wild West stood for the frontier, and the frontier stood for America. The American West was the canvas on which Cody painted his unique and uniquely American portrait. Like any other worthy work of art it continues to be reexamined and reinterpreted.

This current volume is part of that ongoing reexamination. *The Wild West in England*, edited by Frank Christianson, is the fourth volume of The Papers of William F. "Buffalo Bill" Cody and is being published simultaneously with the third volume, *Buffalo Bill from Prairie to Palace* by John M. Burke, edited by Chris Dixon. These two volumes underscore the global nature of Buffalo Bill's Wild West. They document firsthand how, beginning in London in 1887, Buffalo Bill's Wild West performed the drama of frontier settlement to millions of Europeans. They also point to Cody's ability to reach ordinary people and yet appeal to the most elite circles. These new editions give us a clearer picture of a man who transcended geographic, social, cultural, and national boundaries.

We live in a world that is increasingly "flat," where our global economy does not need or even allow unique national identities. Cody had the advantage of operating in a world that delighted in differences and celebrated distinctive identities. Within that context, he posited an uncommon American character and found an energetic reception wherever he went.

To contextualize and better understand that character, the Buffalo Bill Historical Center—its staff, board, and generous supporters—have made a substantial investment in recovering and reclaiming the nineteenth-century American West through its most iconic figure. The William F. "Buffalo Bill" Cody Papers open a window onto a significant national moment—America's coming of age—as documents, photographs, newspapers, and memoirs come into view and reveal a distant but dynamic time and place: the world of Buffalo Bill.

Kurt Graham

EDITOR'S INTRODUCTION

On the final page of his 1879 autobiography, written when he was just thirty-three years old, William F. Cody announces his intention to take his stage play, *The Knights of the Plains*, on a theatrical tour of England the following year. He was concluding this phase of his life story on a high note, reflecting on his considerable success as an actor performing in western melodramas that had toured throughout the United States and identifying the next visible horizon for his ambition. It was eight long years before Cody made it to England, not as a stage actor but on a much grander scale than he could have envisioned as a relatively young man still in transition from plainsman to showman. Cody later acknowledged misgivings that his theatrical production would not be able to distinguish itself enough to generate interest among the English public. In addition, the financing required to make the trip was prohibitive for some years. His early impulse was prescient, however, in identifying England as the arena where he could achieve his greatest success. The 1887–88 season in Britain proved to be a watershed in the history of Buffalo Bill's Wild West, catapulting the show to a new stratum in the world of traveling entertainments and ensuring that it would continue as a cultural force on both sides of the Atlantic for decades to come. *The Wild West in England* recounts the events that led up to the

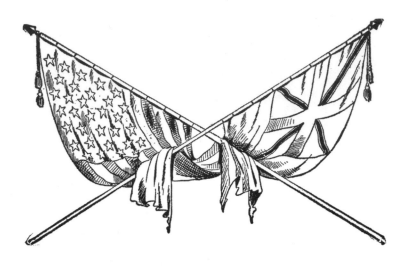

Wild West's transatlantic venture as well as the cultural encounter between American performers and British audiences as it played out during the months of the English tour. Cody's experiences in England take on significance in a broader context of political, economic, and cultural change and provide a singular view of how Americans understood themselves in an increasingly globalized age.

Cody's original autobiography, *The Life of Hon. William F. Cody*, describes his early years in frontier Kansas, including the traumas brought on by the border war and his time in the Union Army. It also traces the stages of his career, from teamster to buffalo hunter to army scout to hunting guide. Beginning in the early 1870s, Cody translated his frontier experience into an acting career by touring the United States with his own theater company, the Buffalo Bill Combination. Both his stage career and his presence as the fictional hero of widely distributed dime novels made Buffalo Bill Cody a household name by 1880. The autobiography offers the raw materials of what became the Buffalo Bill phenomenon, but it concludes before the advent of the Wild West exhibition. *The Wild West in England* picks up the tale where the previous volume left off, detailing Cody's transition from stage to showground. While it offers some specifics regarding the development of Buffalo Bill's Wild West, most of the narrative is devoted to the events of the six-month London season. The text assigns a mythic significance to this unique American export by imagining a historically transformative role for Cody's enterprise. The Wild West stepped onto the global stage as part of an unprecedented effort to market American accomplishments to European audiences in the form of the 1887 American Exhibition.

The Wild West as America's National Entertainment

In 1882, after a decade of touring throughout the United States, William Cody's career as a stage actor was on the wane. A fortuitous meeting in New York with fellow actor-producer Nate Salsbury came at just the right time. Together they developed the rough outlines of a Wild West exhibition centering on horsemanship and marksmanship. From its earliest beginnings, Buffalo Bill's Wild West was imagined as an American cultural export.[1] An 1873 letter to his sister Julia, declaring, "I shall probably go to Europe this fall," reveals that Cody had looked abroad from the very outset of his entertainment career. For his part, Salsbury had already enjoyed considerable success with his own touring company in England and Australia. With this shared ambition, the two men planned to build up investment capital and produce a show for international audiences. A tongue-in-cheek note in the *Detroit Free Press* from December of that year invokes the transatlantic context that gave birth to the Wild West: "Buffalo Bill has at last found a manager willing to take him to England, but what the public will next want to know is whether he is to be left there or not."

Buffalo Bill's Wild West, billing itself as "America's National Entertainment," was meant to originate on English soil. The following spring, however, Cody, impatient to try the concept, broke from the original plan and joined with W. F. "Doc" Carver, a North Platte, Nebraska, dentist and noted marksman, to put together a "Rocky Mountain and Prairie Exhibition." Although the show toured to large audiences throughout 1883, it ended the season without a profit and the partnership between Cody and Carver dissolved in bitterness. *The Wild West in England* ignores this initial period of the show's history, preferring to emphasize the later, more successful, partnership.[2] Cody reconnected with Salsbury and reinvented his exhibition the following year. Although it evolved over time, the basic components of Buffalo Bill's Wild West existed from the beginning. A standard program included racing between cowboys, Mexican vaqueros, and Indians and horsemanship demonstrations, such as the roping and riding of bucking horses, and a Virginia reel on horseback. Marksmanship exhibitions eventually made stars of Annie Oakley, Lillian Smith, and Johnnie Baker. "Illustrations" of Indian attacks on both the Deadwood stagecoach and a settler's cabin, as well as a "genuine buffalo hunt" lent dramatic spectacle to the performance as a whole, as did reenactments of famous battles such as Little Bighorn and Summit Springs. Cody presided over the program, from the opening "Grand Processional" to the final "Salute" and participated in many of the individual events, demonstrating his shooting skills as "America's Practical All-round Shot," repulsing Indian attacks, and staging a mock buffalo hunt.

Native Americans played an integral role in the success of the Wild West, validating the show's claims of authenticity and serving invariably as the aggressors in the show's dramatic set pieces. Cody had employed Indians in some of his first western melodramas in the mid-1870s. Although he had frequently used non-Native actors to play Indians in his stage show, Cody's commitment to casting "real" Indians increased with Buffalo Bill's Wild West, which included as many as one hundred Indians in the cast. Despite the profound ambiguity of their position—staging battles in which they themselves had fought less than a decade after the Plains Indians wars—Indian performers were drawn to both the wages and the opportunity the show provided to travel to new regions of the United States and Europe. Of the many prominent Native Americans involved with the show, Sitting Bull was certainly Cody's greatest recruiting success. His participation for four months during the 1885 season was key to the Wild West's ongoing viability. Sitting Bull's actual performance was a mere cameo role, amounting to a brief ride through the arena and other appearances on the showground. The tour also gave Sitting Bull the opportunity to bypass the standard bureaucratic channels and appeal directly to government officials in Washington DC on behalf of his people.[3] Indian participants such as Standing Bear and Black Elk later wrote about their experiences in the Wild West and reflected a similar mixture of motives for their participation.[4]

Although show cast lists identified Indians from a number of Plains tribes, including Arapahos, Shoshones, and Cheyennes, the show Indians were almost exclusively Sioux. English, and later continental audiences were especially fascinated with the show Indians and the Wild West showcased them to the full. The exhibition of American Natives in Europe had been a tradition since the time of Columbus, but the practice had grown over the course of the nineteenth century. Cody and Salsbury employed the Indians as dramatic foils in one context and as ethnological subjects in another. Audiences were invited to tour the encampment to see how Natives lived; the Wild West program included a scene titled "Phases of Indian Life" in which a "nomadic tribe" recreated a prairie camp and performed Indian dances. Both the ethnography of village life and the melodrama of battle scenes displayed the Indians at their most exotic and spoke to the imperialist impulse, with all its contradictions, among British audiences.

The Wild West in England concludes with a letter of endorsement from Gen. William T. Sherman. A deeply nostalgic Sherman testifies of the authenticity of the Wild West exhibition and catalogs the profound changes that have marked the frontier settlement it portrays, including the replacement of millions of buffalo with cattle and the thousands of Indians with white settlers. While acknowledging the terrible cost of westward expansion, Sherman ultimately calls these changes "salutary" signs that the "laws of nature and civilization" had triumphed, allowing the "earth to blossom as a rose."[5] Sherman's coda reiterates the contradictions that riddle Cody's narrative—in writing and on showground—regarding the status of the Plains Indians. For biographer Louis Warren, Cody's relationship to Native Americans is the most problematic aspect of his legacy: "The real question thus becomes less how Cody derived his sympathies for Indians than how he fashioned a persona of Buffalo Bill that could denounce Indian conquest at one moment and become its most visible advocate in the next. Of all Cody's characteristics, it is this profound ambivalence about

American Indians that seems most impenetrable."[6] Although their place within the Wild West's drama conveyed a variety of meanings to the British press and public, the Indians were indispensable evidence of the Wild West's, and therefore Cody's, authenticity and ultimately its success.

Manifest destiny served as the governing narrative concept that underscored every piece of Wild West spectacle and turned an otherwise loose array of entertainments (much like a circus) into an exhibition of frontier culture that dramatized and justified Anglophone settlement of the American West. The explicitness of this narrative varied with different iterations of the show but found its most coherent expression in the winter season in Madison Square Garden just prior to the 1887 English tour. This revised version of the Wild West, titled *The Drama of Civilization*, offered a linear history of American settlement beginning with the colonies and continuing through to settlement of the far West. At the same time, the Wild West evoked nostalgia for a way of life that was swiftly passing. A mere four years after the English tour, the U.S. Census declared an official end to the American frontier. Cody's exhibition had shrewdly capitalized on a romanticized notion of the West that was nearly extinct. In the three years leading up to the English tour the Wild West polished its presentation and honed the management of its massive logistics. Now billed in promotional materials as "America's National Entertainment," Cody and Salsbury only needed the right circumstances to realize their original vision.

American Exhibitionism

In 1885, English entrepreneur John Whitley conceived of the idea of an exhibition to be staged in the Earls Court district of central London. Officially titled "American Exhibition of Arts, Inventions, Manufactures, & Resources of the United States," the project assembled the best of American achievement in manufacturing, technology, science, and the arts on the model of the world's fairs that had become regular events since the extraordinary success of London's 1851 Crystal Palace Exhibition. However, Whitley altered the standard format, as a description from an official program suggests: "This exhibition will not be an international one," the program claims, "but a new departure . . . being national in character and yet held beyond the limits of the national territory." Whereas most world's fairs offered limited exhibition space for each country, this exhibition devoted its entire focus to one country: the United States. (Whitley later organized similar programs for Italy, France, and Germany.) Originally planned for the summer of 1886, a series of mishaps and delays put the entire privately funded enterprise in jeopardy until Whitley was inspired to invite William Cody and Nate Salsbury to join in on the venture in return for a percentage of the gate receipts. For their part, Cody and Salsbury had already had some experience with a world's fair the previous year in New Orleans at the World's Industrial and Cotton Centennial Exposition. Although the run in New Orleans proved to be a financial failure, the investment, infrastructure, and marketing of the American Exhibition promised to mitigate many of the risks associated with a transatlantic undertaking.

In addition to the financial opportunity, Cody hints at a larger issue involving the development of the Wild West's brand. In *The Wild West in England* he claims that he had been repeatedly urged by "prominent persons of America" to take the show abroad. At least one prominent person was none other than

Mark Twain, who had written Cody three years earlier after attending a performance. Twain lavishes praise on the performance's realism (no small thing coming from one of the founders of American literary realism, who got his start documenting life in the far West), then makes the following claim: "It is often said on the other side of the water that none of the exhibitions which we send to England are purely and distinctively American. If you will take the Wild West show over there, you can remove that reproach." Twain's words reflect a century-long American quest to earn legitimacy in the eyes of the British. Nineteenth-century American cultural history is defined in large part by that effort, and a long list of prominent writers on the subject, including Ralph Waldo Emerson, Henry David Thoreau, Herman Melville, Nathaniel Hawthorne, Walt Whitman, and Henry James, had devoted many pages to the benefits and burdens of America's British cultural inheritance. Twain suggests that American culture-makers labored under the reproach that their work was somehow derivative, and that America's history was too brief, its culture too thin to produce something truly authentic. As Whitman asked of his own country in 1856, "Where are any mental expressions from you beyond what you have copied or stolen?" Whitman countered his own question with a catalog—a rhetorical exhibition, if you will—of American technological and commercial development. His thesis suggests that progress in the arts depends on an infrastructure of publishers, presses, and booksellers to hold its own. He put his faith in "steam power" to erect that infrastructure and finally realize the dream of American cultural independence. In a very literal sense Twain and Cody positioned Buffalo Bill's Wild West as the legatee of earlier nationalist ambitions such as Whitman's.

But what was it about actually going abroad that was so necessary to establishing one's *Americanness*? Twain's own career was marked by both literal and imaginative travel to Europe, paradoxically establishing him as one of the most American-identified and most cosmopolitan men of his generation. In this sense he offered himself as a type to which Cody would also aspire. Both men's careers offer insight into the state of American national identity in the closing decades of the nineteenth century. Twain's appeal to Cody suggests that England is the only setting in which a valid statement of American authenticity can be made. Cody's subsequent performances—in the arena and on the page—draw an inevitable link between America's western (provincial) frontier and the world of cosmopolitan London.

The American Exhibition (nicknamed in the London press "The Yankeeries") opened to the general public on May 9, 1887. According to newspaper estimates, approximately twenty-eight thousand people came to the exhibition on the first day. The main attractions in the American Exhibition included a switchback railway, an early form of roller coaster that carried twenty people in a car on a steeply graded track, as well as a New England toboggan slide and a diorama of New York City viewed from the harbor and featuring the Statue of Liberty. The actual exhibits were less compelling and garnered little notice in the press. From the exhibition grounds patrons could make their way through a causeway to the Wild West encampment and showground laid out on seven acres east of the main Exhibition Hall. Although initial reviews for the exhibition were unenthusiastic in contrast to the generally ecstatic response to the Wild West, a postmortem in the *Times*, published the day after the closing on November 1, portrayed a symbiotic relationship between the exhibition and Cody's show: "The two things, the

Exhibition and the Wild West Show, have supplemented each other. Those who went to be amused often stayed to be instructed. It must be acknowledged that the Show was the attraction which made the fortune of the Exhibition." During the Wild West's six-month London run it routinely played to over twenty thousand visitors (the arena included twenty thousand seats with standing room for ten thousand more) with fourteen performances a week. It was the subject of nonstop coverage in the London press and it welcomed the country's political and cultural elites. Among the more distinguished visitors hosted by Cody were William Gladstone, the once and future British prime minister; Edward, Prince of Wales; and Queen Victoria herself on the eve of her golden jubilee. The Wild West's public relations team expertly incorporated this patronage into its marketing efforts by producing press stories and promotional materials touting "distinguished visitors" with portraits of the queen and company surrounding the central figure of Cody himself (see appendix 3). Indeed, *The Wild West in England* can be viewed as a prose version of these mass-marketed images, exploring every aspect of Cody's success—financial, cultural, even political. From the moment he disembarked, Cody found himself in high demand in London's cultural salons. Invitations poured in from the likes of Henry Irving, London's most celebrated actor, and Oscar and Constance Wilde. Wherever Cody went his outsized persona went with him and his movements within London society became fodder for the press. Whether inside or outside of the arena, Cody and his fellow performers were always on display since the encampment was open to the public and the show's publicity wing made a point of encouraging the headline performers, such as Annie Oakley and Chief Red Shirt, to attend public events where they could garner further media attention.

When the London show came to a close, Cody and Salsbury were able to look back on the most successful season in the four-year history of the Wild West. Approximately two million visitors had paid at least a shilling each to witness the spectacle.[7] Although this financial achievement would be the primary yardstick of success, Cody and company eventually looked to other aspects of the London tour in shaping the Wild West brand for years to come.

From William Cody to Buffalo Bill

When the London season concluded in October, the Wild West traveled north, attempting to replicate the London success with a brief stay in Birmingham at a much smaller venue followed by a five-month winter/spring season in Manchester held in an indoor arena. Cody cites a press account for the detailed description of the Manchester performance, which shows that the Wild West continued to evolve in response to new settings. The Manchester show was more akin to *The Drama of Civilization* performed in Madison Square Garden the previous winter, with its comparatively sophisticated staging. Although attendance was less consistent outside the social and economic hub of London, the northern tour's mixed results did not curtail the air of triumph, which the show carried into New York harbor in May 1888, as it began preparations for a summer season on Staten Island. Later that year the second edition of Cody's autobiography appeared as part of an effort to capture the meaning of the Wild West's international success for American and British audiences. It was included in a collection with biographies of three other people—Daniel Boone, Davy Crockett, and Kit Carson—who together comprised "the renowned pioneer quartette." Entitled *Story of the Wild West and*

STORY of the WILD WEST
AND
CAMP-FIRE CHATS,
BY
BUFFALO BILL,
(HON. W. F. CODY.)

Campfire Chats, the volume listed "Buffalo Bill" as the sole author of all four works. But "Buffalo Bill" had served as Cody's nom de plume prior to 1888, primarily as the putative author of dime novels—dime novels that had been ghostwritten. On one hand, then, using Buffalo Bill as an author name was already an established way of conveying a brand rather than attributing authorship. On the other, when this work is placed alongside the first edition of the autobiography—which credits William Cody—the name Buffalo Bill signals a shift and suggests how Cody's celebrity had evolved. The title of the 1888 edition, *The Autobiography of Buffalo Bill* (in contrast to *The Life of Hon. William F. Cody* in 1879), formally marks the transition and reinforces the idea that the persona had succeeded the person, and the representation the original, in the intervening decade.

In this context, what exactly does authorship mean, when material blurs the conventional boundaries between historical personage (William F. Cody) and celebrity persona (Buffalo Bill)? Since the name Buffalo Bill carried its own kind of authority by this point in Cody's career, the text (*Story of the Wild West*) becomes analogous to the show (*Buffalo Bill's Wild West*). Both *productions* are authorized by the figure of Buffalo Bill, whether exclusively authored by him or not. Cody's life is the source material and expanding his mythic persona is the common objective. In a variation on contemporary publishing terminology, *The Wild West in England* might best be described as an *authorized autobiography*. This formula reframes the question of ultimate authorship by recasting it as just one part of a process of mythmaking.

As if anticipating incredulity from both readers and reviewers, the preface to *Story of the Wild West*, signed by Cody, describes the "study, investigation, and care" he has "devoted to this work." (See appendix 1 for complete text.) After acknowledging his "poor literary qualification," he points to other obstacles for the "sincere" biographer in undertaking such a project. Chief among them is the fact that previous biographies of Boone, Crockett, and Carson have each "made quite as much use of fiction as of actual, verified incident in making up their history of these three prominent characters." He complains that the "idle stories thus incorporated in their work being left so long uncontradicted have become an almost inseparable part of frontier history." While written in a straightforward tone, this statement verges on self-parody and reveals the very process on display in Cody's own autobiography and Wild West show: a process by which "idle stories" become history. Cody inserts himself into this tradition of frontier historiography as

arbiter of the facts and offers a counter to the "wild exaggeration . . . of many romancers." As the primary romancer of his
own life, Cody explicitly aligns Buffalo Bill with his forbears,
both in their renown as legends and as real historical nation-
building figures.

In general outline, *Story of the Wild West* seems to suggest
a standard historical narrative that was popularized just a few
years later by historian Frederick Jackson Turner. The story line
progresses forward in time and further west in space through
each successive legendary figure. Turner promoted the American frontier as a unique site of cultural regeneration, a "meeting
point between savagery and civilization" that placed settlers in
"continuous touch with the simplicity of primitive society" and,
thereby, furnished the "forces dominating American character."[8]
His thesis challenged conventional history, which emphasized
European influence on the development of North America. For
Turner the continuously moving boundary of westward settlement represented the "line of most rapid and effective Americanization."[9] This framework employed the frontier as the foundation of a relentlessly exceptionalist historiography: "The true
point of view in the history of this nation is not the Atlantic
coast, it is the Great West."[10] Turner successfully institutional-
ized a historical narrative that described and enacted America's long-sought-after cultural independence. Although the title page of *Story of the Wild West* gestures to Turner's brand of
frontier boosterism, it also offers itself as evidence to "a wondering world [of] the march of the Anglo-Saxon race towards
the attainment of perfect citizenship and liberal, free and stable government." Cody's version of American history incorpo-
rates an Anglo-Saxon legacy with its emphasis on an essential
relationship among English-speaking peoples. He emphasizes

continuity over difference tying American and European histories together by redirecting the grand narrative of American expansion in its final stage as he heads *east* to England. In Turner's historical vision the further west from the Atlantic seaboard you get, the more American you become. In Cody's ironic inversion, American national identity finds it fullest realization in the expatriate experience. In framing the narrative, Cody addresses Twain's premise: he has staged a singularly American drama in the one place it would matter most, in the *only* place it could legitimately function as a symbol of national exceptionalism. Behind the words in his letter to Cody, Twain probably appreciated the contradictions inherent in finding Americanness in London. But the *Wild West in England* does not reflect a similar consciousness. Cody's closing redirection—from west to east—presents itself as another stage of American cultural conquest and receives its final validation from the crowned heads of Europe: the fountainhead of westward expansionism.

Upon his return to the United States in the spring of 1888, Cody found that his star had risen. Even as he and Salsbury launched another successful season in New York, the *Los Angeles Times* observed that "he is now more talked about in the United States than ever before." His European triumphs granted Cody a new authority with which he could successfully stage his own legend-making. In 1888 Cody joined himself to Boone, Crockett, and Carson as part of the story of the West, and this is what *Story of the Wild West and Campfire Chats* sought to formalize. It is an account of how the idea of the frontier was packaged, sold, and centralized within a broader account of American character. The *Wild West in England* literally concludes *Story of the Wild West* and provides a fitting end for this sweeping account of frontier heroism. It transports the performance of American nationalism to an international stage.

The Frontier Goes Global

Much of the *Wild West in England* is a travel narrative that begins with the Wild West's New York departure on March 31, 1887, and concludes with its return on May 20, 1888. The plot highlights a series of cultural encounters, each charged with a broader significance and each affirming Cody's aspiration that the English tour be "an event of first-class international importance."[11] An early example takes place as Cody's ship nears London in the section titled "Some anxious reflections," which recounts Cody's crisis of self-doubt motivated by his encounter with London as a global commercial hub. As his eyes take in the scene he is overwhelmed by the "crowded waterway with its myriads of crafts of every description, from the quaint channel fishing-boat to the mammoth East India trader and ocean steamers, topped by the flags of all nations, and hailing from every accessible part of the known world, carrying the productions of every clime and laden with every commodity."[12] As Cody experiences globalization first-hand; he tries to imagine a place for his own venture within this new commercial context: "The freight I had brought with me across the broad Atlantic was such a strange and curious one that I naturally wondered whether, after all the trouble, time and expense it had cost me, this pioneer cargo of Nebraska goods would be marketable."[13] Cody's so-called anxious moment helps to frame the narrative that follows: a commercial conquest that Cody sums up only a few pages later when he details the British response to what he calls "American methods of doing business."[14] By this he means the Wild West's formidable logistics, which would soon become legendary.[15] The British are reported to exclaim, "By St. George, the Yankees mean business" in reaction to the organization and scale of the Wild West encampment and arena.[16] The composite Englishman's exclamation is, in essence, the thesis of Cody's story. The Wild West's business success is the rhetorical foundation for all its other achievements, and dramatizing that success becomes the narrative's first priority.

We find a correspondence between commerce and culture in a later episode, wherein Cody uncovers new evidence of an ameliorating spirit between America and Britain: "A walk around the principle streets of London," Cody claims, will show how the Wild West has "'caught on' to the popular imagination. The windows of the London bookseller were full of editions of Fennimore [sic] Cooper's novels." He then lists the titles of Cooper's frontier series "The Leatherstocking Tales," describing them as "those delightful romances which have placed the name of the American novelist on the same level with that of Sir Walter Scott. It was a real revival of trade for the booksellers who sold thousands of volumes of Cooper where 20 years before they had sold them in dozens."[17] Cody uses this evidence to conclude that the Wild West's visit to England has "set the population of the British islands reading, thinking, and talking about their American kinsman to an extent before unprecedented."[18] While 'the sales figures Cody describes may be dubious, his invocation of Cooper is telling. The American novelist would later become the key foil in Mark Twain's attempts to define a new brand of American realism, one shorn of conventions associated with British historical romance. In stark contrast to his praising review of Cody's Wild West, Twain later criticized Cooper's lack of an "observer's protecting gift" that compromised his ability to faithfully represent the American frontier.[19] Cooper's work, then, offers an ambiguous legacy for those who would follow in the tradition of frontier realism. On the one hand he can be seen as a forerunner of Cody (and Twain, for that matter). In the 1820s and 1830s Cooper was among the first of America's transatlantic celebrities. His works imagined the American frontier for a generation of readers. He also left the United States to pursue his career in Europe. But, unlike Cody, he found his relationship to his native country had only become complicated by his time abroad. Cooper found himself and his political sympathies called into question by the American press and he would struggle throughout his career to be seen as an authentic American literary voice. Cody's claim that he is reviving interest in Cooper implies the restoration of a moribund frontier tradition. In celebrating the revival of Cooper's works, Cody is asserting a form of succession: he succeeds where Cooper has not. Cooper, like Walter Scott, was a writer of historical romances; Scott established the tradition and Cooper followed in his wake. Scott would always provide the frame of reference for Cooper because the American wrote in the period of perceived cultural dependence. Cody, also a promoter of historical romances, uses the episode to claim a specific kind of cultural influence. Cody had effectively exported American frontierism as a nationalist ideology where others had failed to do so. By invoking the Leatherstocking books, he identifies in Cooper a cultural genealogy that he purports to transcend.

Cody bolsters his ascendance to nationalist icon in the narrative's climactic scene: a command performance before Queen Victoria on May 11, just days after the exhibition had opened. Although they were forced into canceling a performance to accommodate Queen Victoria's schedule, Cody and Salsbury rightly saw the marketing bonanza afforded by a royal visit to the showground. The autobiography's depiction of the event extends that marketing effort and reveals the most direct insight into the larger objectives of the *Wild West in England*.

Characterizing the performance as one of "unique and unexampled character," Cody raises the stakes by multiple orders of magnitude when he focuses on the opening processional and its ritual of national pageantry, including the presentation of the American flag. Calling it a "notable event" that sent "the blood rushing through every American's veins at Niagara speed," the text imagines a spontaneous expression of respect on the part of the British: "As the standard-bearer waved the proud emblem above his head, Her Majesty rose from her seat and bowed deeply and impressively towards the banner. The whole court party rose, the ladies bowed, the generals present saluted, and the English noblemen took off their hats. Then—we couldn't help it—but there arose such a genuine heart-stirring American yell from our company as seemed to shake the sky. It was a great event."[20] This moment of spontaneous nationalist feeling juxtaposes high and low social ranks to dramatize the triumph of egalitarian sentiment. It emphasizes the ritual aspect of the processional demonstrating the innate power of American iconography.

Cody goes on to place the event within a broader historical context by claiming, "For the first time in history, since the Declaration of Independence, a sovereign of Great Britain had saluted the star spangled banner, and that banner was carried by a member of Buffalo Bill's Wild West! We felt that the hatchet was buried at last and the Wild West had been at the funeral."[21] The comparison is a rich one. In political terms, the Declaration of Independence is America's most dramatic example of exceptionalism. Like *The Wild West in England* it invokes the British monarchy in order to advance a particular version of American identity. But here Cody transforms the Declaration's oppositional logic by receiving the monarch's blessing. Cody's own "declaration" enacts a history-making feat of statesmanship but it does so on his terms. Cody's text carefully emphasizes the convention-bound nature of the command performance, and he is quick to show how the Wild West transgresses those conventions: "As with Mahomet and the Mountain, the Wild West was altogether too colossal to take to Windsor, and so the queen came to the Wild West."[22] The image of a deferential monarch is the culminating moment in Cody's "history."

The British press reported the event quite differently, with a much less demonstrative Victoria simply acknowledging the respectful salute of the performers. And, for her part, the queen's interest seemed to begin and end with the sheer spectacle: "All the different people," she would write in her journal that evening, "wild, painted Red Indians from America, on their wild bare backed horses, of different tribes,—cow boys, Mexicans. &c., all came tearing round at full speed, shrieking, and screaming."[23] Her account of Cody, whom she met personally after the performance, repeats the image projected in the show's own marketing materials. The queen notes that he is "a splendid man, handsome, & gentlemanlike in manner" and is purported to have killed three thousand buffalo "with "many encounters & hand to hand fights with the Red Indians."[24] But for the logic of Cody's narrative, a deferential queen completes the story of the *Wild West in England* as the story of the significance of the frontier in American history. Cody would return to the United States armed with his claims of British conquest and confirmation of his (and Twain's) vision of American cultural independence.

On its surface Cody's account of the command performance seems to be the ultimate example of an "idle story" that shapes the details to advance a larger ideological narrative. At its most brazen it evinces the promotional impulse behind all of Cody's work. However, in the months that followed, the press coverage on both sides of the Atlantic tended to reinforce Cody's claims of extra-commercial ambitions for the Wild West. A *Life* article from May 31, 1888, makes the following argument for the success of the Wild West's nationalist program: "The career of Buffalo William in England ought to teach our Anglomaniacs a useful lesson. The Wild West Show has done more to stimulate Americanism among the republicans who travel abroad, and to inculcate respect for Americans, as Americans, among foreigners, than has ever been accomplished by our ministers at the European courts."[25] At the conclusion of the London season on November 1, 1887, the *Times* of London would actually credit the Wild West with taking the initiative to install an international court of arbitration between the United States and Britain: "At first sight it might seem to be a far cry from the Wild West to an International Court. Yet the connexion is not really very remote. Exhibitions of American products and of a few scenes from the wilder phases of American life certainly tend to some degree at least to bring America near to England. They are partly cause and partly effect. They are the effect of increased and increasing intercourse between the two countries."

Affairs of state notwithstanding, one *effect* of this and similar assessments was the enhancement of an increasingly potent Buffalo Bill mythology. In addition to expanding the arena in which these events played out, the narrative positions Cody in the public eye as both agent and object. Cody embodies ideals of entrepreneurship and masculinity as he confronts a series of challenges with a determination to "pull through," as the text repeatedly puts it. These challenges place Cody as the

WORLD'S WONDROUS VOYAGES

protagonist in a story of epic "conquest" while heightening its scale with each new test. In addition, the narrative represents Cody's achievements through a double lens: his own first-person account and the view from the press box. Cody repeatedly invokes (and, at times, cites at length) newspaper reports of his performance. *The Wild West in England* exhibits Cody as a media celebrity; his selective references to the *London Illustrated News*, the *Sporting Life*, and *Punch*, among others validate his own triumphalism. Ultimately, *Buffalo Bill's Wild West* could return to the United States as something more than entertainment.

As one of its most widely used and iconic show posters suggests, the mere fact of international travel—the mileage count, the routes taken, the sites visited—would become central to the Wild West's claim as America's National Entertainment. Two more extended European tours were still to come, and the show's self-ordained mission of cultural ambassadorship, anchored in a command performance before the queen, was a primary feature of the Wild West brand for the remainder of Cody's celebrated career.

ACKNOWLEDGMENTS

This book owes its existence to Kurt Graham, the founding editor of the Papers of William F. Cody and the editor of the book series. Heather Lundine at the University of Nebraska Press saw the value of the original proposal and encouraged publication. The managing editor of the Papers, Jeremy Johnston, provided research support and offered critical insights on portions of the manuscript. The rest of the Papers team at the Buffalo Bill Historical Center, especially assistant editor Linda Clark, provided essential help in locating and identifying documents and reviewing transcriptions. Key members of that team are Gary Boyce and Deb Adams.

I am indebted to various individuals and entities at Brigham Young University who supported research travel to Cody, Wyoming, and London. In addition to a travel grant from BYU's Kennedy Center for International Studies, I received support from Ed Cutler, chair of the English Department, and John Rosenberg, dean of the College of Humanities. Both department and college also provided research mentoring grants, which gave me the opportunity to work with a number of excellent graduate and undergraduate students on this project. Amy Takabori, Rachel Helps Meibos, and Ben Miller, in particular, conducted research and provided the extra eyes needed to pore over the hundreds of documents located at the McCracken Research

Library and other archives. Mary Robinson and her staff at the McCracken helped make my research trip to Cody extremely productive. Phil Snyder has been an important sounding board and mentor on Cody's legacy, frontier studies, and the nature of autobiography.

The staff at the University of Nebraska Press provided excellent support in preparing the manuscript. History acquisitions editor Bridget Barry oversaw the project from its inception. Ann Baker offered surefooted editorial feedback and expertly steered the manuscript through copyediting and production.

Along with the professional support of my colleagues, the emotional resources I need to complete just about anything I do come from my team in Provo: Stace and the girls—Quinnie, Tealie, and Maggie.

A NOTE ON THE TEXT

Although the names William F. Cody and Buffalo Bill have been attached to many works of both fiction and nonfiction, the question of Cody's authorship has always been contested with regard to any work not written in his own handwriting. A consensus appears to have emerged among historians that Cody's 1879 autobiography reflects his own voice, but the same cannot be said for the second edition as it appeared in the 1888 book, *Story of the Wild West*. Even had he had the inclination to become a biographer, it seems obvious that Cody could not have written the other three frontier biographies, given the demands on his time in 1887 and 1888.[1] An examination of the *Autobiography of Buffalo Bill*, as the second edition is titled, reveals a significant abridgment: most of the material from the later work is drawn from the original, but it is condensed from thirty-two chapters in the 1879 edition to twenty-two in the subsequent one. New material is limited to a handful of illustrations; some, such as the image of a bloody scalp, added to the text's sensational appeal.

The Wild West in England is listed not as an additional chapter in the table of contents but as a separate work appended to the end of the autobiography. With the exception of a scattering of newspaper publications, this addendum would be the only new autobiographical writing attributed to Cody after the 1879 edition. While many scholars cite the work to Cody without disclaimer, some have questioned the degree to which Cody participated in both the editing of the original text and the composition of the new material. Cody had nearly an extra decade behind him after his last foray into life writing, and it is certainly possible that his own voice had developed a greater sophistication during those years. However, a more distant and elevated tone, as well as more frequent use of historical and cultural allusions, reflects an extra layer of editorial intervention. Louis Warren, in *Buffalo Bill's America* (2005), has notably attributed authorship to Cody's public relations manager, John Burke. The text's promotional air suggests that Burke, if not a full coterie of pressmen, had a hand in developing the narrative, even if many original anecdotes and observations came from Cody. In listing "Buffalo Bill" as the author, the publisher suggests an association with a brand rather than a literal claim of exclusive authorship. Whatever Cody's degree of involvement in drafting the text, *The Wild West in England*, like countless dime novels and the Wild West show itself, is a Cody enterprise. It exists to promote a version of his public persona that advances his broader mass marketing program.

The University of Nebraska Press edition is based on the 1888 edition of *The Wild West in England* as it was published in *Story of the Wild West and Campfire Chats*. The volume of frontier biographies appeared in multiple editions that year, from presses such as Historical Publishing Company of Philadelphia, R. S. Peale of Chicago, and Eastern Publishing of Boston. The three were part of an emerging industry in subscription books sold door to door and in mail-order catalogs. Most editions list an H. S. Smith as the copyright holder. Variations among the 1888 editions are limited to the phrasing of a few sentences and the inclusion of the General W. T. Sherman letter of endorsement at the end of the volume. The decision to include the Sherman letter, as well as which phrasings to feature, was based on the most common usage among the various available versions. No handwritten document associated with this text exists. Silent emendations have been made where spelling is a matter of consistency or as a matter of accuracy with regard to known historical figures. The "List of Scenes" in this edition conforms to the first edition. In some cases the phrasing in the list varies from that of the title in text. In other cases there is no corresponding title.

The appendixes include material from the 1880s, with special emphasis on the period of the English tour. The photographs and memorabilia are a representative fraction of the material available in collections on the Cody Digital Archive and at the Buffalo Bill Historical Center's McCracken Research Library.

The Wild West in England

WILLIAM F. CODY

LIST OF SCENES

An Ambitious Enterprise—Opening of the Wild West Show—Nate Salsbury Joins Me as a Partner—A Sketch of Salsbury's Active Life—A Bigger Show Put on the Road—The Show Is Dumped into the Mississippi—Our Losses in New Orleans—A Season in New York—A Hazardous Undertaking—Seeking New Worlds to Conquer—We Sail for England—The Indians' Fears Are Excited—A Sea-sick Troupe—Off Gravesend—An Enthusiastic Welcome to England—Some Anxious Reflections—First Impressions of London—Preparing the Exhibition Grounds—Scenes on the Strand—Steaming up the Thames—Establishing our Camp—Queer Scenes—The Starry Flag Raised in England—American Methods Excite Surprise—Henry Irving's Generous Praise—A Wild West Performance Described—Helpful Influence from Distinguished Persons—Enthusiastic and Numerous Social Courtesies—Entertained by the Greatest of London—How the Press Treated Me—The Poetic Muse Honors Me—The Coming Centaur—Visit of Mr. Gladstone—A Private Performance in His Honor—His Complimentary Speech—A Hard Worked Lion of the Season—The Grand Dinner Given Me—Visit of the Prince and Princess of Wales—A Private Entertainment for His Royal Highness—The Many Royal Persons Present—Their

Unqualified Praise Bestowed—Immense Excitement Created in London—Our First Public Performance—The Wild West Show—Interest Without Bloody Accessories—Visit of Her Majesty, Queen Victoria—Etiquette of Invitation—Her Majesty Salutes the American Flag—Presented to the Queen—Expressions of Her Queenly Favor—Statesmen at the Wild West—A Ribroast Breakfast to Gen. Simon Cameron—The Prince of Wales and His Royal Flush—A Wondrous Scene and Kingly Event—Royalty Taking a Ride on the Deadwood Coach—Kings, Queens, Princes, Dukes, Lords and Ladies take in the Show—Presented with a Diamond Pin by the Prince of Wales—The Princess of Wales Rides in the Deadwood Coach—Her Visit to the Show in cognito—A Word of Praise from the London Times—Kind Words, Kind Feelings and Kind Friends on Every Side—Departure for the Provinces—A Visit to Italy—Re-opening in Manchester—The Mammoth Building Erected for our Exhibition—A Grand Description of our Show in Manchester—The Crowd at our Opening Performance—Social Honors Heaped Upon Me—Presented with a Rifle—A Jolly Occasion—The Ribroast of Pa He-Haska—English Love of Sport Illustrated—Presented with a Gold Watch by Citizens—Streets in Salford Named in My Honor—A Magnificent Ovation—A Benefit Given Me by the Race-course People—50,000 People Present—A Race for $2500—An Enthusiastic Farewell—Sailing for New York—A Pathetic Incident at Sea—Reception upon Our Arrival at New York—The Joy of Stepping upon the Soil of Dear America Again—Happy Meeting with Friends

THE WILD WEST IN ENGLAND

When the season of 1882–83[1] closed I found myself richer by several thousand dollars than I had ever been before, having done a splendid business at every place where my performance was given in that year. Immense success and comparative wealth, attained in the profession of showman, stimulated me to greater exertion and largely increased my ambition for public favor. Accordingly, I conceived the idea of organizing a large company of Indians, cow-boys, Mexican vaqueros,[2] famous riders and expert lasso-throwers, with accessories of stage coach, emigrant wagons, bucking horses and a herd of buffaloes, with which to give a realistic entertainment of wild life on the plains. To accomplish this purpose, which in many respects was a really herculean undertaking, I sent agents to various points in the far West to engage Indians from several different tribes, and then set about the more difficult enterprise of capturing a herd of buffaloes. After several months of patient work I secured the services of nearly fifty cowboys and Mexicans skilled in lasso-throwing and famous as daring riders, but when these were engaged, and several buffaloes, elk and mountain sheep were obtained, I found all the difficulties had not yet been overcome, for such exhibitions as I had prepared to give could only be shown in large open-air enclosures, and these were not always to be rented, while those that I found suitable were often inaccessible by such popular conveyances as street cars. The expenses of such a show as I had determined to give were so great that a very large crowd must be drawn to every exhibition or a financial failure would be certain; hence I soon found that my ambitious conception, instead of bringing me fortune, was more likely to end in disaster. But having gone so far in the matter I determined to see the end whatever it might be.

In the spring of 1883 (May 17th)[3] I opened the Wild West Show at the fairgrounds in Omaha, and played to very large crowds, the weather fortunately proving propitious. We played our next engagement at Springfield, Ill., and thence in all the large cities, to the seaboard.[4] The enterprise was not a complete financial success during the first season, though everywhere our performances were attended by immense audiences.

NATE SALSBURY JOINS ME AS A PARTNER

Though I had made no money at the end of the first year, the profit came to me in the way of valuable experience and I was in no wise discouraged. Flattering offers were made me by circus organizations to go on the road as an adjunct to their exhibitions, but I refused them all, determined to win success with my prairie Wild West Show or go down in complete failure. The very large patronage I received during my first season convinced me that if I could form a partnership with someone capable of attending to the management and business details that the enterprise would prove a magnificent success, a belief which I am glad to say was speedily realized.

My career on the stage threw me in contact with a great many leading stars, and I came to have an acquaintanceship with nearly all my contemporary American actors. Among those with whom I became most intimate was Nate Salsbury,[5] a comedian whose equal I do not believe graces the stage of either America or England today. Aside from his popularity and wealth, acquired in legitimate comedy, I knew him to be a reliable friend, and withal endowed with a rare business sagacity that gave him the reputation of being one of the very best, as well as successful, managers in the show business. Knowing

4. Nate Salsbury.

his character as such, I approached him with a proposition to join me as an equal partner, in putting the Wild West entertainment again on the road. The result of my overtures was the formation of a partnership that still continues, and under the new management and partnership of Cody & Salsbury, the Wild West has won all its glory.

The reader will pardon a digression from the general scope of this autobiography for the probably more interesting, though all too brief, allusion to the career of my esteemed partner, who has won success in life by struggles quite as difficult and trying as any through which I have passed.

Nate (Nathan) Salsbury was born in Freeport, Ill., in 1846, when his parents were in such humble circumstances that his early training was all in the direction of "digging sand and sawing wood." As there was little to bind his affections to the home of his nativity, when the war broke out Nate joined the Fifteenth Illinois, with which he remained, as a private in the ranks, sixteen months. In 1863 he again enlisted and participated in a dozen battles and was wounded three times. His career as an active participant was terminated by his capture and incarceration in Andersonville prison,[6] where he remained subjected to all the horrors of that dreadful pen for a period of seven months. Being at length exchanged[7] he returned home and entered the law office of Judge Beck, now Chief Justice of Colorado, with the idea of becoming a lawyer. A few months of office study and attendance at commercial school only served to impress him with the idea that the profession would still have a fairly large membership even though his name were not added to the list. Abandoning his former expectations he went to school for a time and in the class exhibitions and amateur theatricals of his town developed a desire to go on the stage.

The first experience Nate had in search of a crown for his greatest ambition was far from a pleasant one. Having saved up less than a score of dollars he went to Grand Rapids, Mich., and there made application of the Opera House managers, Johnson, Oates & Hayden, for a situation. Mr. Oates asked him his line of business to which Nate modestly replied, "Oh, anything." "Well," said Oates, "what salary do you expect?" "Oh, anything," was the equally prompt response. Seeing that the applicant had evidently not yet passed the threshold of the profession, Oates said to him, in an indifferent manner. "I will give you twelve dollars a week and you'll be d—d lucky if you get a cent." He didn't; but he entered the profession, which was the next best thing.

From Grand Rapids Nate went to Detroit, where he remained three months without advancing himself either financially or professionally. Somewhat discouraged he returned to his Illinois home, but only to stay a few months, when his restless ambition prompted him to try his fortune in the East. Accordingly he went to Baltimore, and thence to Boston, where he secured a situation at the Boston Museum[8] with a salary of twelve dollars per week. Here his talent was soon discovered by the management, who raised his salary to twenty-eight dollars per week. Others also saw the budding genius of Nate and after playing a season at the Museum he accepted the position of leading heavy man at Hooley's theater in Chicago.

His progress thenceforward was rapid, as his popularity grew apace and his salary rose with every new engagement. But there was too much originality in the man to permit of him remaining a member of a stock company,[9] so at the conclusion of his second season at Hooley's he conceived and constructed a comedy entertainment, with eight people in the cast, to which he gave the title of "The Troubadours." For twelve years this organization, as originally formed, with very slight changes, continued on the road and played repeatedly in all the largest cities with splendid success.

Following "The Troubadours," Nate wrote another comedy, called "Patchwork," which had a run of eighteen months, and then he brought out his most successful comedy, "The Brook," which he wrote entire in eight hours, and at a single sitting. This piece he played continuously for five years, making a large amount of money and pleasing millions of people, until he joined me and took the active management of the Wild West Show, which compelled him to withdraw from the stage.

A BIGGER SHOW PUT ON THE ROAD

Immediately upon forming a partnership with Salsbury[10] we set about increasing the company and preparing to greatly enlarge the exhibition. Nearly one hundred Indians, from several tribes, were engaged, among the number being the world famous Chief Sitting Bull,[11] and several other Sioux that had distinguished themselves in the Custer massacre.[12] Besides these we secured the services of many noted plainsmen, such as Buck Taylor, the great rider, lasso thrower and King of the Cowboys; Utah Frank, John Nelson, and a score of other well-known characters.[13] We also captured a herd of elk, a dozen buffaloes and some bears with which to illustrate the chase.

5. Sitting Bull.

THE SHOW IS DUMPED INTO THE MISSISSIPPI

Our vastly enlarged and reorganized company gave daily exhibitions in all the large cities to enormous crowds during the summer of 1884, and in the fall we started for New Orleans to spend the winter exhibiting at the Exposition Grounds.[14] We accordingly chartered a steamer to transport our property and troupe to the Crescent City. Nothing of moment transpired on the trip until we were near Rodney Landing, Miss., when our boat collided with another and was so badly damaged that she sank in less than an hour. In this accident we lost all our personal effects, including wagons, camp equipage, arms, ammunition, donkeys, buffaloes and one elk. We managed, however, to save our horses, Deadwood coach, band wagon, and—ourselves. The loss thus entailed was about $20,000.

As soon as I could reach a telegraph station I hastily sent a telegram to Salsbury, who was with the Troubadours at Denver, as follows: "Outfit at bottom of the river, what do you advise?" As I learned afterwards, Salsbury was just on the point of going upon the stage to sing a song when my rueful telegram was handed him. The news hit him hard, but in no wise disconcerted him; stepping to the speaking tube connecting with the orchestra he shouted to the leader, "Play that symphony again and a little louder, I want to think a minute." As the music struck up he wrote out the following message: "Go to New Orleans, reorganize and open on your date," which I received and promptly complied with his instructions.

In eight days I had added to the nucleus that had been saved a herd of buffalo and elk, and all the necessary wagons and other properties, completing the equipment so thoroughly that the show in many respects was better prepared than at the time of the accident—and we opened on our date.

A SEASON IN NEW YORK

The New Orleans exposition did not prove the success that many of its promoters anticipated and the expectations of Mr. Salsbury and myself were alike disappointed, for at the end of the winter we counted our losses at about $60,000.

The following summer we played at Staten Island, on the magnificent grounds of Mr. Erastus Wiman,[15] and met with such splendid success that our losses at New Orleans were speedily retrieved. So well satisfied were we with New York that we leased Madison Square Garden[16] for the winter of 1886-87 and gave our exhibition there for the first time in a covered space. We gave two performances every day during the entire winter and nearly always played to crowded houses, though the seating capacity of the place was about 15,000.

AN AMBITIOUS BUT HAZARDOUS UNDERTAKING

The immortal bard has well said, "ambition grows with what it feeds on."[17] So with Salsbury and I, our unexampled success throughout America with the Wild West show excited our ambition to conquer other nations than our own. Though the idea of transplanting our exhibition, for a time, to England had frequently occurred to us, the importance of such an undertaking was enlarged and brought us to a more favorable consideration of the project by repeated suggestions from prominent persons of America,[18] and particularly by urgent invitations extended by distinguished Englishmen. While inclined to the enterprise we gave much thought to the enormous expense involved in such a step and might not have decided so soon to try the rather hazardous experiment but for an opportunity that promised to largely increase our chances of success.

Several leading gentlemen of the United States conceived the idea of holding an American Exhibition in the heart of London[19] and to this end a company was organized that pushed the project to a successful issue, aided as they were by several prominent residents of the English capital. When the enterprise had progressed so far as to give flattering promise of an opening at the time fixed upon, a proposition was made to Mr. Salsbury and myself,

6. Capturing Bear for the Exhibition.

by the president and directors of the company, to take our show to London and play the season of six months as an adjunct of the American Exhibition, the proposition being a percentage of the gate receipts.

After a mature consideration of the offer we accepted it and immediately set about enlarging our organization and preparing for a departure for England.

A great deal of preliminary work was necessary, but we set manfully about the task of securing the services of a hundred Indians, representative types of the Sioux, Cheyenne, Kiowa, Pawnee and Ogalallas tribes, and succeeded in getting the required number, none of whom had ever been off their reservations prior to joining my show. Among the prominent chiefs thus engaged was Red Shirt,[20] a redoubtable warrior and second only in influence to Sitting Bull himself. A short while before his engagement with us he had quelled an uprising among his people, instigated by a pretender to the chieftainship of the tribe, by invading the pretender's camp with only two of his followers and shooting the leader dead before the eyes of his affrighted wife. This fearless act had served to elevate him very much in the eyes of his people, who thereafter accepted him as a leader. When, therefore, he decided to join the Wild West show, under the flattering offers I made him, his influence aided us very much in procuring our complement of Indians, not only from his own tribe, but from others as well.

SEEKING NEW WORLDS TO CONQUER

Our arrangements having at length been completed, by collecting together a company of more than two hundred men and animals, consisting of Indians, cowboys, (including the celebrated Cowboy band),[21] Mexican wild riders, celebrated rifle shots, buffaloes, Texas steers, burros, bronchos, racing horses, elk, bears, and an immense amount of camp paraphernalia, such as tents, wagons, stage coach, etc., we chartered the steamship State of Nebraska, of the State line, Capt. Braes, and were ready to set sail to a country that I had long wished to visit,—the Motherland. Accordingly, on Thursday, March 31st, 1887, we set sail from New York, the piers crowded with thousands of our good friends who came down to wave their adieux and to wish us a pleasant voyage. Our departure was an occasion I shall never forget, for as the ship drew away from the pier such cheers went up as I never before heard, while our Cowboy band played "The Girl I left Behind Me" in a manner that suggested more reality than empty sentiment in the familiar air. Salsbury and I, and my daughter Arta,[22] waved our hats in sad farewells and stood upon the deck watching the still cheering crowd until they faded in the distance, and we were out upon the deep, for the first time in my life.

7. Red Shirt Killing His Rival.

THE INDIANS' FEARS ARE EXCITED

Before starting on the trip several of the Indians expressed grave fears that if they trusted themselves to the great waters a horrible death would soon overtake them, and at the last moment it required all our arts of persuasion to induce them to go on board.

Red Shirt explained that these fears were caused by a belief prevalent among many tribes of Indians, that if a red man attempted to cross the ocean, soon after beginning his journey he would be seized of a malady that would first prostrate the victim and then slowly consume his flesh, day after day, until at length the very skin itself would drop from his bones, leaving nothing but the skeleton and this even could never find burial. This gruesome belief was repeated by chiefs of the several tribes to the Indians who had joined me, so that there is little reason for wonder, that with all our assurances, the poor unlearned children of a nature run riot by neglect, should hesitate to submit themselves to such an experiment.

On the day following our departure from New York the Indians began to grow weary and their stomachs, like my own, became both treacherous and rebellious. Their fears were now so greatly intensified that even Red Shirt, the bravest of his people, looked anxiously towards the

8. Our Departure for England.

hereafter, and began to feel his flesh to see if it were really diminishing. The seal of hopelessness stamped upon the faces of the Indians aroused my pity, and though sick as a cow with hollow-horn myself, I used my utmost endeavors to cheer them up and relieve their forebodings. But for two days nearly the whole company was too sick for any other active service than feeding the fishes, in which I am not proud to say that I performed more than an ordinary share. On the third day, however, we all began to mend so far that I called the Indians together in the main saloon and gave them a Sunday address, as did also Red Shirt, who was now recovered from his anxiety about the future.

After the third day at sea we had an entertainment every afternoon, in which Mr. Salsbury, as singer and comedian, took the leading part, to the intense delight of all on board. On the seventh day a storm came up that raged so fiercely that for a time the ship had to lay to, and during which our stock suffered greatly, but we gave them such good care, and had such excellent luck as well, that none of our animals, save one horse, died on the trip.

"OFF GRAVESEND"

At last as we cast anchor off Gravesend[23] a tug boat approaching attracted the entire company on deck, for we were expecting to meet our advance manager, Jno. M. Burke,[24] with general instructions as to our landing, etc. It turned out, however, to be a government boat loaded with custom-house and quarantine officials, under whom we were to pass the usual inspection. Another official accompanied them, with whom arrangements had been made for the passage of our arms, as a restriction was placed upon the landing of our ammunition, of which we had brought a large quantity, the English government regulations requiring that it be unloaded and turned over to the arsenal authorities, in whose charge it was kept during our stay in London, we drawing on them daily for our supply as needed. I feel in duty bound to acknowledge here that the English government, through its different officials, extended to us every kind of courtesy, privileges and general facilities that materially assisted in rendering pleasant the last few hours of a remarkable voyage. The bovines and buffalo that were a part of our outfit were inspected, and a special permit granted us to take them to the Albert dock, the place of our debarkation, and after holding them in quarantine there for a few days they were allowed to join us in camp.

Recent disastrous outbreaks of rinderpest, foot and mouth disease, and other ills that bovine flesh is heir to, necessitate the law being very strict as regards importation of cattle, all foreign beasts being required to be killed within twenty-four hours after their arrival.

SOME ANXIOUS REFLECTIONS

During this delay time was given me for reflection and gradually as my eyes wandered over the crowded waterway with its myriads of crafts of every description, from the quaint channel fishing-boat to the mammoth East India trader and ocean steamers, topped by the flags of all nations and hailing from every accessible part of the known world, carrying the productions of every clime and laden with every commodity, I thought of the magnitude of the enterprise I was engaged in and wondered what its results would be.

The freight I had brought with me across the broad Atlantic was such a strange and curious one that I naturally wondered whether, after all trouble, time and expense it had cost me, this pioneer cargo of Nebraska goods would be marketable. In fact, it would take a much more facile pen than mine to portray the thick crowding thoughts that scurried through my brain. Standing on the deck of a ship, called the "State of Nebraska," whose arrival had evidently been watched for with great curiosity, as the number of yachts, tug boats and other crafts which surrounded us attested, my memory wandered back to the days of my youth, when in search of the necessaries of existence and braving the dangers of the then vast wild plains, a section of which comprised the then unsettled territory of Nebraska. I contrasted that epoch of my life, its lonely duties and its hardships, and all its complex history, as the home and battle-ground of a savage foe, with its present great prosperity and its standing as the empire State of the central West. A certain feeling of pride came over me when I thought of the good ship on whose deck I stood, and that her cargo consisted of early pioneers and rude, rough riders from that section, and of the wild horses of the same district, buffalo, deer, elk and antelope— the king game of the prairie,—together with over one hundred representatives of that savage foe that had been compelled to submit to a conquering civilization and were now accompanying me in friendship, loyalty and peace, five thousand miles from their homes, braving the dangers of the to them great unknown sea, now no longer a tradition, but a reality—all of us combined in an exhibition intended to prove to the center of old world civilization that the vast region of the United States was finally and effectively settled by the English-speaking race.

OUR RECEPTION IN ENGLAND

This train of thought was interrupted by the sight of a tug with the starry banner flying from her peak bearing down upon us, and a tumultuous waving of handkerchiefs on board, evoking shouts and cheers from all our company.

As the tug came nearer, strains of "The Star Spangled Banner," rendered by a band on her deck, fell upon our ears, and immediately our own Cowboy band responded with "Yankee Doodle," creating a general tumult on our ship as the word was passed from bow to stern that friends were near. Once alongside, the company on board the tug proved to be the directors of the American Exhibition, with Lord Ronald Gower[25] heading a distinguished committee accompanied by Maj. Burke and representatives of the leading journals, who made us feel at last that our sea voyage was ended.

FIRST IMPRESSIONS OF LONDON

After the usual introductions, greetings and reception of instructions, I accompanied the committee on shore at Gravesend, where quite an ovation was given us amid cries of "Welcome to old England" and "three cheers for Bill," which gave pleasing evidence of the public interest that had been awakened in our coming.

A special train of saloon carriages was waiting to convey us to London and we soon left the quaint old Kentish town behind us, and in an hour we arrived at Victoria station. The high road-bed of the railroad, which runs level with the chimney tops, was a novel sight, as we scurried along through what seemed to be an endless sea of habitation, and I have scarcely yet found out where Gravesend finishes and London commences, so dense is the population of the suburbs off the "boss village" of the British Isles, and so numerous the small towns through which we passed. The impression created by the grand Victoria station, by the underground railroad, the strange sights and busy scenes of the "West End," the hustle and the bustle of a first evening view of mighty London, would alone make a chapter.

My first opinion of the streets was that they were sufficiently lively and noisy to have alarmed all the dogs in every Indian village in the Platte country, from the Missouri river to the headwaters of the Platte, in its most primitive days.

A short trip on the somewhat dark and sulphurous underground railroad[26] brought us to West Kensington, a quiet section of the West End, the station of which had been already connected by special bridges, then nearly completed, with the grounds as yet unknown to London, but destined to become the scene of several months' continuous triumphs. Entering the headquarters of the exhibition we found a bounteous repast set and a generous welcome accorded us. The heartiness of my reception, combined with the natural sense of relief after such a journey and the general indications of success, proved a happy relaxation of the nervous strain to which I had been subjected for several weeks. Speeches, toasts and well wishes, etc., accompanied the spirited and spirituous celebration of the occasion. My genial hosts' capacity for the liquid refreshments would have made me envy them in the 60s, and led me to suspect that there might be accomplishments in England in which even western pioneers are excelled.

PREPARING THE EXHIBITION GROUNDS

After brief social converse, and a tranquilizing smoke, we made a casual visit to the grounds, where the preparations for the stabling, the arena and the grand stand, with busy hundreds of workmen hastening their completions by night by the aid of *lucigen* lights[27] and bon-fires, presented an animated scene, and a display of energy rarely witnessed in connection with an amusement enterprise. These operations were dealing with the expenditure of $125,000, including the fencing in of an arena more than a third of a mile in circumference, flanked by a grand stand filled with seats and boxes, estimated to accommodate 20,000 persons. Sheltered stands for 10,000 more were also being erected; it being understood that room for 40,000 spectators in all should be provided at each performance. For the Indian encampment a large hill had been thrown up by spare labor, and this was already decorated by a grove of newly planted trees. The stables for horses, mules and mustangs, and the corrals for buffaloes, antelope, elk, etc., were all in simultaneous course of construction. Everything so far impressed me very favorably and I began to feel that if we did not command success we would, with our advantages of location, surroundings and novelty and realism, at least deserve it.

The interest evinced by the British workmen in my presence detracting somewhat from their attention to business, caused us to retire after a brief inspection. This same curiosity however was as a straw indicating which way the wind blew. I was now, for the first time, introduced in its own habitat to that world-famed vehicle, the London hansom cab.[28] In one of them I was whirled through the West End, past the famous Hyde Park, through Piccadilly, around Leicester and Trafalgar squares, to that central resort and theatrical hub of this vast community, the Strand.[29] This narrow street, in its relation to the great city, reminded me of one of the contracted passes in the "Rockies," to which traffic had been naturally attracted, and usage had made a necessity. The density of its foot traffic, the thronging herd of omnibuses, the twisting, wriggling, shouting, whip-cracking cabbies, seemed like Broadway squeezed narrower, and I realized at once the utility and necessity of the two-wheeled curio in which I was whirled through the bewildering mingle of Strand traffic. With but one or two hub-bumps we were soon landed at the magnificent hotel Metropole, in Northumberland avenue, where I met many American gentlemen from different cities, who recognized me on sight and gave me hearty greeting. I retired early, determined to retrace my steps to Gravesend at daylight and ascend the Thames on board the Nebraska, as my great anxiety was the successful debarkation.

STEAMING UP THE THAMES

Steaming up on an early tide, which at its flood I now felt certain would lead on to fortune, and with flags flying, we entered amid a perfect ovation the great port of London. The short trip made on that bright morning was one of great pleasure to all on board. The ship's officers pointed out the many sites of historical interest, as we steamed past them, such as the Old Tillbury Fort, facing Gravesend, erected by Henry the Eighth, and memorable as the place where Queen Elizabeth reviewed her troops after the destruction of the Spanish Armada.[30] Woolwich and its mighty arsenals and gun factories; Greenwich with its grand old Naval College, now used as a free hospital for *sick seamen of all nations*, in front of which stands the obelisk erected to the dauntless explorer, Billot, at the back of it the emerald hills of the Old Park, topped by the observatory which supplies the correct time—all of these engaged our attention in turn. As we moved slowly up the tideway, the huge fleets of sea-going vessels became more crowded; forests of masts and spars stretching away seemingly in illimitable perspective, while on our starboard side the extensive docks in an endless series spoke of the majesty of commerce and the overflowing glories of what Englishmen only call "The Port of London." This magnificent revelation reminded me of a remark made by an English gentleman on the street, who said, "we may not be very large geographically, but we are gigantic commercially."

My attention was especially attracted by a movable crane in the center of one great basin taking up a car containing 20 tons of coal and emptying it in the hole of a ship in a few seconds.

ESTABLISHING OUR CAMP— A QUEER SCENE

With the assistance of our horsemen, each looking after his own horse, we were unloaded with a rapidity that astonished even the old dock hands and officials. Through the courtesy of the custom house people, there was hardly a moment's delay in the process of debarkation, but although landed in London, we were still twelve miles from our future camp. So, quickly loading our entire outfit on three trains we were very speedily delivered at the Midland railway depot, almost adjoining our grounds, and by four o'clock that afternoon the horses were in the stables, watered, fed, and bedded, camp equipage and bedding distributed; our own regular camp cooks were hastening a meal; tents were going up, stoves being erected, tables spread and set in the open air; tepees rapidly erected, and by 6 o'clock a perfect canvas city had sprung up in the heart of West-End London.

The halliards[31] of the flag staff raised the starry banner to the breeze, and as the Cowboy band rendered our national air a storm of shouts and cheers went up from the thousands that lined the walls, streets and housetops of the surrounding neighborhoods. This was very gratifying, and in answer to these hearty plaudits we gave them "God Save the Queen," and so The Wild West and

BUCK TAYLOR
KING OF THE COWBOYS.

RED SHIRT
FIGHTING CHIEF OF THE SIOUX

WA-KA-CHA-SHA
THE PET OF THE SIOUX.

THE ENCAMPMENT.

Bill Cody, of Nebraska, U. S. A., "was at home in camp in London." The first domestic episode (our camp-meal being necessarily eaten in full view of our kindly neighbors, the large dining tents not yet being up), was as novel to them, from our variegated and motley population of Indians, cowboys, scouts, Mexicans, etc., and eminently practical method of "grubbing," as the supply of fresh beef, mutton, corn-bread, ham, etc., *l'Americaine* was grateful to our sea-faring palates. The meal was finished by seven o'clock, and by 9 p.m. the little camp was almost as complete as if it had been there for months, and its tired occupants, men, women and children, were reposing more snugly and peacefully than they had done in many weeks.

AMERICAN METHODS OF DOING BUSINESS EXCITE FAVORABLE SURPRISE

Trivial as these details may appear at first sight, the rapidity with which we had transported our stuff from dock to depot, and depot to grounds, and made our camp as above related, had an immense effect. The number of notable visitors present, representatives of the press and the well-to-do people of the neighborhood, expressed surprise and astonishment, and communicated the same feeling to the whole of London. It was generally remarked, "By St. George, the Yankees mean business." As we had several days before the opening there were plenty of opportunities given me to receive the many distinguished persons who called, and whom I afterwards found so friendly and hospitable. Mr. Henry Irving, who had witnessed our performance at Staten Island, and who had kindly assisted in the most generous manner to pave the way for our success, was among the first to offer his kindly offices and lent us a strength of public, professional, personal, and social influence that to me was almost invaluable.[32] He had already, long before our arrival, spoken of us in the kindest terms to a representative of the *Era,* the principal dramatic organ of London; and I may here take the liberty of quoting a portion of his highly sympathetic remarks:

Henry Irving's Generous Praise

"I saw an entertainment in New York the like of which I had never seen before, which impressed me immensely. It is coming to London, and will be exhibited somewhere near Earl's Court, on the grounds of the forthcoming American Exhibition. It is an entertainment in which the whole of the most interesting episodes of life on the extreme frontier of civilization in America are represented with the most graphic vividness and scrupulosity of detail. You may form some idea of the scale upon which the scene is played when I say that when I saw it the stage extended over five acres. You have real cowboys, with bucking horses, real buffaloes, and great hordes of cows, which are lassoed and stampeded in the most realistic fashion imaginable. Then there are real Indians, who execute attacks upon coaches driven at full speed. No one can exaggerate the extreme excitement and 'go' of the whole performance. However well it may be rehearsed—and the greatest care is taken that it shall go properly—it is impossible to avoid a considerable share of the impromptu and the unforeseen. For you may rehearse with buffaloes as much as you like, but no one can say in what way they will stampede when they are suddenly turned loose in the open. No one can say how the ox has to be lassoed, or in what way the guns have to be fired when the border fight comes on. The excitement is immense, and I venture to predict that when it comes to London it will take the town by storm."

A writer in the same journal had published the following lively description of our doings at Erastina, Staten

Island. I place this article here as an evidence of the good-natured way in which the English press had prepared the public mind for our coming, and a partial explanation of the avidity with which our opening day was looked for:

A Wild West Performance

"In the grove of Erastina, is the Wild West encampment, adjoining the exhibition grounds. It is not unlike a military camp, with its headquarters under canvas, and its grouped tepees savagely ornamented with scalps and feathers. The picturesque Indian children playing under the trees, the uncouth, extemporized comfort and the prevailing air of organization give it a novel interest. There are no restrictions upon visitors, who are allowed to enter the tents, chuck the Indian babies under the chin, watch the squaws at work, and interview the patriarchal chief who sits grim and stoical on his blanket. Of the exhibition on the grounds (and the proprietors will not allow you to call it a performance), especially at night when lit by the electric lights, the wild beauty of it is an entirely new element in our arena sports. When I saw it there were by gate record 12,000 people on the stands, which you will understand is the population of a goodly town. A stentorian voice in front of the grand stand makes the announcements, and as he does so, the bands make their entry from the extreme end of the grounds, dashing up to the stand, a third of a mile, at a whirlwind pace. As an exhibition of equestrianism nothing in the world can equal this. Pawnees, Sioux, Cut Off Band, Ogalallas, cowboys, make this dash in groups, successively, and pull up in a growing array before the stand 200 strong. Such daredevil riding was never seen among Cossacks, Tartars, Arabs. All the picturesque horsemanship of the famous Bedouins sinks to child's play before these reckless Mamelukes[33] of the plains. When the American cowboys sweep like a tornado up the track, forty or fifty strong, every man swinging his hat and every pony at his utmost speed, a roar of wonder and delight breaks from the thousands, and the men reach the grand stand in a cloud, welcomed by a thunderburst. Col. Cody, the far-famed Buffalo Bill, comes last. I don't know that anybody ever described Buffalo Bill on a horse. I am inclined to think nobody can. Ainsworth's description of Dick Turpin's ride stood for many years as the finest thing of its kind,[34] and then young Winthrop in his clever story of 'John Brent' excelled it in his ride to the Suggernell Springs.[35] Either one of these men, given a month and a safe publisher, might have wrought Buffalo Bill upon paper. He is the complete restoration of the Centaur. No one that I ever saw so adequately fulfills to the eye all the conditions of picturesque beauty, absolute grace, and perfect identity with his animal. If an artist or a riding master had wanted to mould a living ideal of romantic equestrianship, containing in outline and action the men of Harry of Navarre,[36] the Americanism of Custer, the automatic majesty of the Indian, and the untutored cussedness of the cowboy, he would have measured Buffalo Bill in the saddle. Motion swings into music with him. He is the only man I ever saw who rides as if he couldn't help it and the sculptor and the soldier had jointly come together in his act. It is well worth a visit to Erastina to see that vast parterre of people break into white handkerchiefs, like a calm sea suddenly whipped

10. Our First Evening Performance—by the Electric Light—in London.

to foam, as this man dashes up to the grand stand. How encumbered, and uncouth and wooden are best of the red braves beside the martial leadership of this long-limbed pale-face! There they are, drawn up in platoon front. No circus can approximate its actuality. Look down the line. Every man has a record of daring, and there, shaking her long hair, is Georgie Duffie, the Colorado girl.[37] A word of command, the line breaks. Away they go with shouts and yells. In an instant the grounds are covered with the vanishing hoofs. Feathers and war-paint glimmer in the mad swirl and they are gone in the distance. It is impossible to escape the thrill of this intense action. The enthusiasm of the multitude goes with them. All the abeyant savagery in the blood and bones comes to the surface, and men and women shout together. An impression prevailed among some of the spectators that these wild bucking horses are trained after the manner of circus horses. Nothing can be further from the truth, as I had occasion to learn after staying at the camp for two or three days and making their acquaintance. They are simply wild horses spoiled in the breaking. There is one black mare they call Dynamite that is, without exception, the wickedest animal I ever saw. You are to understand that when a man attempts to mount her she jumps into the air, and turning a back somersault, falls upon her back with her heels upward. To escape being crushed to death is to employ the marvelous celerity and dexterity that a cowboy alone exhibits. The other day a cowboy undertook to ride this animal. It was necessary for four men to hold her and she had to be blindfolded before he could get on her, and then, letting out a scream like a woman in pain, she made a headlong dash and plunged with all her force into a fence, turning completely over head first and apparently falling upon the rider. A cry of horror rose from the spectators. But the rest of the exhibition went on. Poor Jim was dragged out, bleeding and maimed, and led away. What was the astonishment of the multitude, when the other refractory animals had had their sport, to see Dynamite again led out and the cowboy, limping and pale, came forward to make another attempt to ride her. 'No, no,' cried the spectators, 'take her away.' But the indomitable cowboy only smiled grimly and gave them to understand that in the cowboys' code a man who failed to ride his animal might as well retire from business. It was do or die. For fifteen minutes the fight went on between man and beast. Animal strength against pluck and intelligence. I never saw a multitude brought to such intense interest. It was the gladiatorial contest revived. The infuriated beast shook off the men who held her like insects. She leapt into the air with a scream and fell on her back. She laid down and grovelled. But the cowboy got upon her back by some superhuman skill, and then he was master. As he punished the animal mercilessly and swung his hat triumphantly, the concourse of people stood up and cheered long and loud."

HELPFUL INFLUENCE FROM DISTINGUISHED PERSONS

Not only England's greatest actor living but his old friend the genial Jno. L. Toole, Miss Ellen Terry, Mr. Justin McCarthy, M. P., Minister Phelps, Consul-General Gov. Thos. Waller, Deputy Consul Moffat (to whom we are greatly indebted for assistance rendered us in landing), Mr. Henry Labouchere, Miss Mary Anderson, Mrs. Brown-Potter, Mr. Chas. Wyndham, and in fact all of the prominent members of the theatrical profession, and the literati in general, seemed to take an immense and friendly interest in our enterprise. Lord Ronald Gower, Sir Cundiffe Owen, Lord Henry Pagett, Lord Charles Beresford, the Grand Duke Michael of Russia, who was an early jubilee[38] visitor, Lady Monckton, Sir Francis Knollys, private secretary to the Prince of Wales, Colonel Clark, Colonel Montague, Lady Alice Bective, whom the Indians presently named "The sunshine of the camp," Lord Strathmore, Lord Windsor, Lady Randolph Churchill, Mrs. J. W. Mackay, a host of distinguished American residents of London and hundreds of other prominent personages, visited the camp and stables before the regular opening, and by their expressions of friendship and good-will gave us the greatest encouragement for the future.[39]

It thus became increasingly evident to me that we

had struck a responsive chord in the heart of all Londoners. The sight of the Indians, cowboys, American girls, and Mexicans living in their primitive simplicity, was very attractive to them, while the innate English love of horsemanship and feats of skill presaged an appreciative community which I must say from the first to last never disappointed us. In fact, it may be said we commenced business with a strong predisposition of all Englishmen to be pleased with us if we gave the public anything at all approaching the surprising novelty of brilliant realism they had been led to expect. The press were generous to us to an extent possibly never before known. Its columns were teeming daily with information about us, so eulogistic that I almost feared we would not come up to expectations. Twenty-five scrap books filled to repletion with such notices now adorn my library and as a sample I insert these few, of varied form, to show how the subject of the day was variously treated. The *London Illustrated News* of April 16, in connection with a two page illustration and four columns of descriptive matter, is drawn upon for the following extract:

How the Press Treated Me

It is certainly a novel idea for one nation to give an Exhibition devoted exclusively to its own frontier history or the story enacted by genuine characters of the dangers and hardships of its settlement upon the soil of another country three thousand miles away. Yet this is exactly what the Americans will do this year in London, and it is an idea worthy of that thorough-going and enterprising people. We frankly and gladly allow that there is a natural and sentimental view of the design which will go far to obtain for it a hearty welcome in England. The progress of the United States, now the largest community of the English race on the face of the earth, though not in political union with Great Britain, yet intimately connected with us by social sympathies, by a common language and literature, by ancestral traditions and many centuries of a common history, by much remaining similarity of civil institutions, laws, morals and manners, by the same forms of religions, by the same attachment to the principles of order and freedom, and by the mutual interchange of benefits in a vast commerce and in the materials and sustenance of their staple industries, is a proper subject of congratulation; for the popular mind, in the United Kingdom, does not regard, and will never be taught to regard, what are styled "Imperial" interests—those of mere political dominion—as equally valuable with the habits and ideas and domestic life of the aggregate of human families belonging to our own race. The greater numerical proportion of these, already exceeding sixty millions, are inhabitants of the great American Republic, while the English-speaking subjects of Queen Victoria number a little above forty-five millions, including those in Canada and Australasia and scattered among the colonial dependencies of this realm. It would be unnatural to deny ourselves the indulgence of a just gratification in seeing what men of our own blood, men of our own mind and disposition, in all essential respects, though tempered and sharpened by more stimulating conditions, with some wider opportunities for exertion, have achieved, in raising a wonderful fabric of modern civilization, and bringing it to the highest prosperity, across the whole breadth of the Western Continent, from the Atlantic to the Pacific Ocean. We feel sure that this sentiment will prevail in the hearts of hundreds of thousands of visitors to Buffalo Bill's American camp, about to be opened at the West End of London; and we take it kindly of the great kindred people of the United States, that they now send such a magnificent representation to the Motherland, determined to take some part in celebrating the Jubilee of her Majesty the Queen, who is the political representative of the people of Great Britain and Ireland.

The tone of this article strikes the same chord, I may say, as the whole of the comments of the English press. It divested the Wild West of its attributes as an entertainment simply, and treated our visit as an event of first class international importance, and a link between the affections of the two kindred nations, such as had never before been forged. Following it came a very flattering description of the site of our operations:

A large covered bridge, crossing the railway, leads eastward to the grounds near Earl's Court Station, where will be located "Buffalo Bill's" Wild West Exhibition. The preparations for the reception of this unique entertainment have been very extensive; they were made under the supervision of Major J. M. Burke, the general manager of the "Wild West." The track is over one-third of a mile in circumference, and within this is the arena. It is flanked by a grand stand filled with seats and boxes, which will accommodate twenty thousand persons. Standing room under shelter is provided for over ten thousand more, and this, with the spectators in the open, will give a good view of the entertainment to about forty thousand people. A large hill has been thrown up of earth and rocks; and on this, amidst a grove of newly-planted trees, will be the encampment of the Indians, the "cowboys," and scouts. At the other side of the grounds are extensive stables for the broncho horses and mules, and a corral for the buffaloes, antelopes, elk, and other wild animals. This remarkable exhibition, the "Wild West," has created a furor in America, and the reason is easy to understand. It is not a circus, nor indeed is it acting at all, in a theatrical sense; but an exact reproduction of daily scenes in frontier life, as experienced and enacted by the very people who now form the "Wild West" company. It comprises Indian life, "cowboy" life, Indian fighting, and burning Indian villages, lassoing and breaking in wild horses,

12. Scenes in the Wild West Show.

shooting, feats of strength, and border athletic games and sports. It could only be possible for such a remarkable undertaking to be carried out by a remarkable man: and the Hon. W. F. Cody, known as "Buffalo Bill," guide, scout, hunter, trapper, Indian fighter, and legislator, *is* a remarkable man. He is a perfect horseman, an unerring shot, a man of magnificent presence and physique, ignorant of the meaning of fear or fatigue; his life is a history of hairbreadth escapes, and deeds of daring, generosity, and self-sacrifice, which compare very favorably with the chivalric actions of romance, and he has been not inappropriately designated the "Bayard of the Plains."

It may seem a little egotistical to present this last sentence to the reader's notice, but as I am free to confess pleasure at the generous allusion to my country and myself, I feel the reader will forgive me, if the result to him or her should be the sinking of any fragment of thoughtless prejudice and the building up of a feeling of reciprocal appreciation. Personally, I feel of course, that I was simply the accidental opportunity for the expression of latent kindly feeling from the sons of our ancestors—political countrymen. The journals seemed to vie with each other in varied expressions of cordial welcome, which took the form of lengthy eulogy, pictorial and editorial description, comic and poetic effusions, as *vide*[40] the following excerpts. Here speaks the *Referee:*

The Poetic Muse Is Evoked

Buffalo Bill

South Kensington's lustre is waning,
The Westminster fun's getting stale;

The star of the Battenbergs' setting,
  The Parnellite comet grows pale.
The Crawford-Dilke scandal's[41] forgotten,
  The Law Court sensations are nil;
Society needs a new tonic,—
  So come along, Buffalo Bill.

We hear that the cowboys are wonders,
  And do what no rough-rider dare,
So wherever the "pitch" is in London
  Its wild horses *will* drag us there.
O, fancy the scene of excitement!
  O, fancy five acres of thrill,
The cowboys and Injuns and horses,
  And the far-famed Buffalo Bill!

They say he's a darling, a hero,
  A truly magnificent man,
With hair that falls over his shoulders,
  And a face that's a picture to scan;
And then he's so strong and so daring,
  Yet gentle and nice with it still—
Only fancy if all the young ladies
  Go mashed upon Buffalo Bill!

The world is a wearisome desert,
  The life that we live is a bore;
The cheek of the apple is rosy,
  But the canker-worm hides in the core,
Our hearts have a void that is aching—
  That void, then, O, hasten to fill
With your mustangs and Injuns and cowboys,
  And yourself, O great Buffalo Bill!

Punch appeared with your humble servant pictured as a centaur, with bull-whip and revolver, and the annexed stanzas:

The Coming Centaur

Midst cheering tremendous,
O'er valley and hill—
A marvel stupendous
Of courage and skill—
He's quickly advancing,
With singing and dancing
That Centaur Heroic called Buffalo Bill.

Soon he'll cross the Atlantic,
In quest of new game,
With horses half frantic
And riders the same:
A novel sensation
He'll make in this nation—
So cheers half a hundred for Buffalo Bill!

With horsemanship daring
Our sight will be blest;
All the town will be staring
At sports of the West.
His American cowboys
Will kick up a row boys,
Such as London will witness with rapturous zest.

This Centaur Heroic
Would gladden a Stoic,
So droll is his humor,
so curious his skill.
We'll get something sunny
And fresh for our money
Hip! hip! hip! hooray! then, for Buffalo Bill.

VISIT OF MR. GLADSTONE—PRIVATE VIEW BY THE GRAND OLD MAN

We were yet in the throes of our extensive preparations, and the backward English spring was getting in its work with a saddening, soddering supply of surplus fresh water, when I received intimation that the ex-Premier, the Right Hon. W. E. Gladstone, M. P., intended to honor the Wild West with a preliminary call.[42] This visit was fixed for the 25th of April, and although worried almost to death with the exertions connected with "rounding up," I determined to make the veteran statesman's call as pleasant as possible, although, as the track was not completed, a full show could not be given. Shortly after one o'clock p.m. he arrived at Earl's Court with Mrs. Gladstone, and entered the grounds in company with the Marquis of Lorne (husband of the Princess Louise), attended by Lord Ronald Gower, Mr. Waller (Consul General of the United States), and a distinguished party, escorted by Nate Salsbury. The Cowboy band welcomed the visitors with the strains of "Yankee Doodle," and I presently had the pleasure of shaking hands with and introducing Mr. and Mrs. Gladstone to the denizens of our encampment. The fine old statesman, looking like intellect personified, glanced around him with an amused expression as the savage Indians came flocking out with their characteristic cries of "ugh,

13. Scenes in the Amphitheater.

ugh" and engaged at once in conversation with Red Shirt. I explained to the gallant Sioux warrior that Mr. Gladstone was one of the great white chiefs of England, and they were soon on excellent terms. The ex-Premier puzzled him exceedingly, however, by inquiring, through our interpreter, if he thought the Englishman looked enough like the Americans to make him think they were kinsmen and brothers. Red Shirt set us all laughing by replying that "he wasn't quite sure about that." It was clear that the red man hadn't studied the art of compliment to any great extent, but the incident passed off good humoredly enough and the party left the camp for the grand stand. Their astonishment, when the Indians in full war paint, riding their swift horses, dashed into the arena from an ambuscade, knew no bounds, and the enthusiasm grew, as placing myself at the head of the whole body, I wheeled them into line for a general salute. Then the lasso, our feats of shooting, and the bucking horses were introduced, and it was a real treat to see the evergreen ex-Premier enjoying himself like a veritable schoolboy, as the American cowboys tackled the incorrigible bucking horses, sometimes cheering the animal, sometimes the man. At the finish he assured me he could have conceived nothing more interesting or amusing.

A luncheon followed in the exhibition building at which I sat beside Mrs. Gladstone. The Grand Old Man spoke in warm and affecting terms of the instrumental good work we had come to do. He proposed "success to the Wild West Show" in a brilliant little speech which aroused the enthusiasm of all present. He was highly complimentary to America and dwelt upon the great deeds of its western pioneers in a glowing peroration, and on subsequent occasions, when we met, his demeanor was such that I could quite understand the fascination he exercises over the masses of his countrymen. His is a singularly attractive personality and his voice is either a balm to comfort or a living sword, two-edged and fire tipped, for the oratorical combat as occasion may demand. Consul-General Thos. Waller responded effusively and I began to feel that I was really becoming a factor, in my humble way, in the great task of cementing an international good feeling.

A HARD-WORKED LION
OF THE SEASON

Then commenced a long series of invitations to breakfasts, dinners, luncheons, and midnight lay-outs, garden parties and all the other attentions by which London society delights to honor what it is pleased to call the distinguished foreigner. I began to feel that life is indeed sometimes too short to contain all the gayety that people would fain compress into its narrow limits. A reference to my diary shows that amongst other receptions I visited and was made an honorary member of most of the best clubs. Notably the Reform Club, where I met the Prince of Wales, the Duke of Cambridge, and a coterie of prominent gentlemen. Then came a civic lunch at the Mansion House with the Lord Mayor and Lady Mayoress; a dinner at the Beaufort Club, where that fine sportsman, the Duke of Beaufort, took the chair; and a memorable evening at the Savage Club, with Mr. Wilson Barrett (just back from America) presiding, and an attendance comprising such great spirits as Mr. Henry Irving, John L. Toole, and all that is great in literary, artistic and histrionic London; at the United Arts Club I was entertained by the Duke of Teck; and at the St. George's Club, by Lord Bruce, Lord Woolmex, Lord Lymington, Mr. Christopher Sykes, Mr. Herbert Gladstone and others;

subsequently I dined at Mr. Irving's, Lady McGregor's, Lady Tenterden's, Mrs. Chas. Matthews, (widow of the great actor), Mrs. J. W. Mackay's, Lord Randolph and Lady Churchill's, Edmund Yates's, and at Great Marlow; also with Mrs. Courtland Palmer, U.S. Minister Phelps, and again at the Savage Club with Gov. Thos. Waller. Then came invites from Mrs. J. Tandell Phillips, the Hon. Cecil and Mrs. Donovan, Mr. and Mrs. Brandon; from Chas. Wyndham, at the Criterion; from Mr. Lawson, of the *Daily Telegraph*, to meet the Duke of Cambridge. I was dined also at Lady Monckton's, Mr. and Mrs. Oscar Wilde's; the Burlingham Club, Mme. Minnie Hauk de Wartegg's, Lady Ardelsun's, Miss Mary Anderson's, an enthusiastic Wild Wester, Emma Nevada Palmer's, and at Mrs. Brown Potter's, who was very active in personal interest. I visited Mr. Henry Labouchere on the occasion when Mr. and Mrs. Labouchere gave their grand garden production of "A Midsummer Night's Dream." Then I remember riding in great style with Lord Chas. Beresford in the Coaching Club parade in Hyde Park, and received an invitation to a mount with the Hon. Artillery Co. of London (the oldest volunteer in the kingdom), in the parade in honor of Her Majesty's the Queen's birthday. This last, business prevented my accepting. These are but a few among the many social courtesies extended to me, all of which I shall forever appreciate and remember with the greatest pleasure.[43] But I must say that, considering my pre-occupation with our preliminary arrangements, and the social demands made upon my time, it is now a wonder to myself how I succeeded in forming so good an exhibition at the opening day. It should be remembered that the Indians were all new from the Pine Ridge Agency, and had never seen the exhibition, and that a hundred of the ponies came direct from the plains of Texas and had never been ridden or shot over.

VISIT OF THE PRINCE AND PRINCESS OF WALES

Amidst all of this fashionable hurly-burly, I was extremely gratified to receive the following letter:

Marlborough House,
Pall Mall, S. W., 26 April, 1887.

Dear Sir: I am desired by the Prince of Wales to thank you for your invitation. His Royal Highness is anxious I should see you with reference to it. Perhaps, therefore, you would kindly make it convenient to call at Marlborough House.

Would it suit you to call at 11:30 or 5 o'clock, either to morrow (Wednesday) or Thursday? I am, dear sir.

Yours faithfully,
(Signed) *Francis Knollys,*
Private Secretary

This resulted in an arrangement to give a special performance for H. R. H. the Prince and Princess of Wales, although everything was still incomplete, the track unfinished, spoiled by rainy weather and the hauling on of vast timbers. The ground was in unspeakably bad condition.

The Prince of Wales being busily occupied in arranging matters for the Queen's Jubilee, had but limited latitude as regard to time. But for all this I determined to pull through, as the Wild West always suited me the more raw and wild it was. I retired the night previous to the visit fatigued to be sure, but with a hunter's pleasant reflections after striking a country where water is plenty and grazing good, two circumstances that always bring the weary pioneer renewed confidence and repose.

A PRIVATE ENTERTAINMENT FOR THE PRINCE OF WALES

The entertainment was of course to be an exclusive one, confined entirely to the royal party, as it yet wanted several days to an opening date. I had got the royal box handsomely rigged out with American and English flags, and my object was to make use of the occasion as a further rehearsal of the whole entertainment. The party that was conducted into our precincts was a strong one numerically as well as in point of exalted rank: The Prince and Princess of Wales, with their three daughters, Princesses Louise, Victoria and Maud, led the way; then came the Princess Louise and her husband, the Marquis of Lorne; the Duke of Cambridge; H. S. H. of Teck and his son; the Comtesse de Paris; the Crown Prince of Denmark; followed by Lady Suffield and Miss Knollys, Lady Cole, Colonel Clarke, Lord Edward Somerset and other high placed attendants on the assembled royalties. The Prince of Wales introduced me to the Princess, and introductions to the other exalted personages followed, in which Nate Salsbury and Major John Burke were included. His Royal Highness is under the medium height and rather inclined to corpulency. In manners mixed with that indescribable high bearing which comes from constant association with state ceremonial, he is just the *beau ideal* of a plain-spoken, pleasant,

LILLIAN SMITH. ANNIE OAKLEY. A SQUAW ATTACK ON THE DEADWOOD COACH. A SQUAW

kindly gentleman. He takes the universal homage as a matter of course; but never acts as though he would exact it. I had the pleasure of meeting him many times subsequently, and found less pride in him than I have experienced in third-rate civic officials elsewhere.

Before I left London he presented me with a very handsome diamond copy of his crest—the three ostrich feathers—mounted in gems and gold as a breast-pin. But of that more anon. The Princess of Wales is a quiet, self-possessed, gentle lady, much given to innocent merriment, and still speaking English with a slightly-clipped foreign accent. My knowledge of the state of the arena and the nervous feeling inseparable from a first performance made me anything but comfortable as I conducted my guests in their boxes, and left them in charge of Major Burke and Mr. Frank Richmond,[44] who had the task of explaining the various acts in the performance. However, we were in for it and were bound to pull through, and my fears of a mishap were dispelled from the moment the Prince gave the signal, and the Indians, yelling like fiends, galloped out from their ambuscade and swept round the enclosure like a whirlwind. The effect was instantaneous and electric. The Prince rose from his seat and leaned eagerly over the front of the box, and the whole party seemed thrilled at the spectacle. "Cody," I said to myself, "you have fetched 'em!" From that moment we were right—right from the word "Go." Everybody was in capital form—myself included—and the whole thing went off grandly. Our lady shots, on being presented at the finish, committed the small solecism of offering to shake hands with the Princess; for be it known that feminine royalty offers the hand back uppermost, which the person presented is expected to reverently lift with the finger tips and to salute with the lips. However, the Princess got over the difficulty by taking their proffered hands and shaking them heartily.

Then came an inspection of Indian camp, and a talk between the Prince and Red Shirt. His Royal Highness expressed through the interpreter his great delight at what he had seen, and the Princess personally offered him a welcome to England. "Tell the Great Chief's wife," said Red Shirt with much dignity, "that it gladdens my heart to hear her words of welcome." The Royal party *cottoned* greatly to John Nelson's half-breed papoose, and while the ladies of the suite were petting the baby the Prince honored my headquarters tent with a visit and seemed much interested in the gold-mounted sword presented to me by the generals of the United States Army with whom I have served in the boisterous years that are never to return.

15. An Introduction to the Prince and Princess of Wales.

The Prince of Wales is an earnest sportsman and a bold rider to hounds. That I knew, but I was a little surprised when, in spite of the muddy state of the ground, he and his party determined to make an inspection of the stables where our 200 broncho horses and other animals were quartered. I never felt prouder of the military method that pervades our equine arrangements than during this visit, which was sprung upon me quite as a surprise. All was in apple-pie order and everybody seemed exceedingly pleased.

He quite won my heart by demanding the full, true and particular history of Old Charlie, now in his twenty-first year, who carried me through so much arduous work in the plains, and who once bore me over a flight of 100 miles in nine hours and forty minutes when chased by hostile Indians. Charlie may not have felt the compliment, but I appreciated it keenly.

And so at seven o'clock our royal visit and our first full performance in England terminated by the prince presenting the contents of his cigarette case to Red Shirt. The rehearsal had been a triumphant success and we had earned the approval of the first gentleman in the land. It may be imagined how heartily Nate Salsbury, Major Burke, and I congratulated each other on this auspicious issue of a big occasion.

A walk round the principal streets of London at this time would have shown how by anticipation the Wild West had "caught on" to the popular imagination. The windows of the London bookseller were full of editions of Fenimore Cooper's novels, "The Path-Finder," "The Deer Stalker," "The Last of the Mohicans," "Leather Stocking," and in short, all that series of delightful romances which have placed the name of the American novelist on the same level with that of Sir Walter Scott.[45] It was a real revival of trade for the booksellers, who sold thousands of volumes of Cooper where twenty years before they had sold them in dozens. I am convinced—and I say it in no boast-ful spirit, but as a plain statement of fact—that our visit to England has set the population of the British Islands reading, thinking, and talking about their American kins-men to an extent before unprecedented. They are begin-ning to know more of the mighty nation beyond the At-lantic and consequently to esteem us better than at any time within the limits of modern history. I am proud of my small share in this desirable state of things, which will be a source of comfort to me to my dying day.

OUR OPENING PERFORMANCE

A glorious change in the weather. Sunny skies and balmy breezes ushered in the morning of May 9, and the stars and stripes fluttered and glittered above us in the warm, soft air as if rejoicing in the good fortune that was to come. The happy omen was realized in the shape of a bumper attendance. The moment the doors were opened there was a great rush of the populace, and our money-takers had all their work cut out, "with both hands," to relieve the bustling perspiring crowd of the harmless necessary shillings that flowed in silver streams into our coffers. It was a thoroughly representative audience, fashionable and otherwise, in which all ranks were included; and if I had felt slightly nervous in the presence of royalty, I experienced a sensation of real stage fright on gazing at the vast sea of faces that confronted us from every available quarter when we made our first bow to the British public. A cutting from an influential London paper may be allowed to describe the scene:

The Wild West Show

As we took our places in one of the little boxes which edge the arena in the grounds of the American Exhibition where Buffalo Bill's Wild West Show is given, we could not help being struck with the effectiveness of the scene before us. The size of the enclosure was one element of the impressiveness of the *coup dœil*[46] and this was cleverly increased by the picturesque scenery which enclosed half of the circle. At the edge of the ash-covered circle in the center were drawn up on parade the whole strength of the Wild West company. There were the various tribes of Indians in their war-paint and feathers, the Mexicans, the ladies, and the cowboys, and a fine array they made, with the chiefs of each tribe, the renowned Sergeant Bates,[47] the equally celebrated Buffalo Bill, the stalwart Buck Taylor, and others who were introduced by Mr. Frank Richmond who, from the top of an elevated platform, described the show as it proceeded. The post of lecturer is no sinecure when such a vast area has to be filled by the voice of the speaker; but Mr. Richmond made every sentence distinctly heard, and the interesting information conveyed by him in a mellow and decidedly audible voice was one of the most agreeable features of the performance. Few, perhaps, of the audience would have remembered, without the notification of the lecturer, the history of the pony express, one of the most romantic in the annals of intercommunication, or have enjoyed fully the exposition by one of the leading cowboys of the way in which the mails were carried. The emigrant train, which next wended its way across the arena with its teams of oxen and mules, its ancient wagons, and their burden of families and household goods, to be attacked by a tribe of redskins, who were soon repulsed by the ever ready cow-boys, was an equally interesting resurrection of a method of peopling the soil practiced even

16. Buck Taylor Riding an Eruptive Mustang.

now in the remoter regions of the West, though the red-skins, we believe, are pretty well confined nowadays to the Indian territory, and are reduced to, at least, an outward "friendliness." The next sensation was created by Miss Lillian Smith, "the California girl," whose forte is shooting at a swinging target. She complicates her feats by adding all kinds of difficulties to her aim, and her crowning achievements of smashing a glass ball made to revolve horizontally at great speed and clearing off ball after ball on the target just mentioned to the number of twenty were really marvelous. The part of the entertainment most novel to Londoners was undoubtedly the riding of the "bucking" horses.

As Mr. Richmond explained, no cruelty is used to make these animals "buck." It is simply "a way they've got." The horses are saddled *coram publico*,[48] and the ingenious manœuvres by means of which this is accomplished were extremely interesting to observe. Some escaped altogether from their masters, and had to be pursued and lassoed; others had to be thrown down in order that they might be mounted. When the cowboys were in the saddle came the tug of war. There were various degrees of violence in the leaps and springs of the animals, but the mildest of them would have thrown even a moderately good rider to the ground in a moment. The "ugliest" of the lot seemed to be that bestridden at the conclusion of this part of the show by Antonio Esquival, but those mounted by Jim Kidd, Buck Taylor, Dick Johnson, Mitchell, and Webb[49] were all "customers" of the "awkwardest" description, and showed what a rebellious demon there is in a half-broken horse who has lost his fear of man. There was enmity, savage or sullen, in every attitude and in every movement of these creatures. The bucking horses should be seen by everyone in London who takes an interest in the "noble animal." The attack on the Deadwood stage coach,[50] which is a celebrated item of the show, was a very effective spectacle, and in this, as in an attack on a settler's homestead, there was a great amount of powder burnt. Mustang Jack performed the startling feat of clearing a horse sixteen hands high, having previously covered thirteen feet with a standing leap. He is, without doubt, an extraordinary jumper. Buffalo Bill's specialty is shooting whilst riding at full gallop, and he does this to wonderful perfection. He is accompanied by an Indian, bearing a basket full of glass balls, which he throws high into the air, and Mr. Cody smashes each with unerring aim whilst both horses are going at a hard gallop. The buffalo hunt was immensely realistic. There was also some interesting feats, riding by two ladies and several short races between them, and also between Indian boys mounted on mustang ponies. Summing up the Wild West show from an English and theatrical point of view, we should say that it is certain to draw thousands from its remarkably novel nature. We would also suggest for consideration the advantage of the introduction of a little scalping. Why should not the Indians overcome a party of scouts, and "raise their hair?" Wigs and scalps are not very expensive, and carmine is decidedly cheap. But it will be a long time before public curiosity will be glutted, and until then "Buffalo Bill" may be content to "let her rip," and regard with complacency the golden stream that is flowing with such a mighty current into the treasury of the Wild West Show.

INTEREST WITHOUT BLOODY ACCESSORIES

The drawback to the exploiting of this ingenious idea is that a display of sham scalping would by no means satisfy gentlemen of this reporter's gory turn of mind. Nothing but a real massacre, with genuine blood flowing and a comfortable array of corpses for view would suffice to glut some people's appetite for a nice, thrilling sensation. Perhaps if the gentleman had ever seen the horrors of actual warfare with red Indians he would not be so zealous for realism. However, he meant well, and his pen was but one amongst the hundreds wielded by English journalists who shed ink in kindly praise of our endeavors to amuse and instruct the London public. Another critic, he of the *Sporting Life*, concludes a whimsical notice in laudatory terms thus:

> The opening of the Wild West Show was one of the most signal successes of recent years. Such a vast concourse of the cream—or it may be as well to say the *creme de la crème*—of society is seldom seen at any performance. The number of chariots waiting at the gates outnumbered those of Pharaoh, and the phalanx of footmen constituted quite a small army. There is much in the Wild West

show to please. There is novelty of incident, wonderful tone, color, dexterous horsemanship, and a breezy independence of manner, which latter quality, by the way, is not entirely confined to the *dramatis personæ*. It is new, it is brilliant, it is startling, it will "go!"

VISIT OF QUEEN VICTORIA

"By command of Her Majesty, the Queen"—it must be understood, that the Queen never requests, desires, or invites, even her own Prime Minister to her own dinner-table, but "commands" invariably—a special performance was given by the Wild West, the understanding being that Her Majesty and suite would take a private view of the performance. The Queen, ever since the death of her husband, nearly thirty years ago, has cherished an invincible objection to appearing before great assemblages of her subjects. She visits her Parliament seldom; the theaters never. Her latest knowledge of her greatest actors and actresses has been gained from private performances at Windsor, whither they have been "commanded" to entertain her, and that at very infrequent intervals. But as with Mahomet and the mountain,[51] the Wild West was altogether too colossal to take to Windsor, and so the Queen came to the Wild West—an honor of which I was the more deeply sensible on account of its unique and unexampled character. I am bound to say that the whole troupe, myself included, felt highly complimented; the public would hardly believe it, and if bets had been made at the clubs, the odds on a rank outsider in the Derby would have been nothing to the amount that would have been bet that it was a Yankee hoax. Her Majesty would arrive, I was informed, at five o'clock, and would require to see everything in an hour. A soldier is frequently ordered to accomplish the impossible—I had been tolerably used to that sort of thing, and have knocked the impossible stiff and cold on more than one occasion; but this was a poser. We would do our best and acquit ourselves like men and women; and that was all that could be said about it. We erected a dais for Her Majesty and had a box specially constructed, draped with crimson velvet and decorated with orchids, leaving plenty of accommodation for the attendant notables. All was made as bright and cheerful as possible, and these preparation's completed we waited, very much in frame of mind like a lot of school boys attending an examination.

HER MAJESTY SALUTES THE AMERICAN FLAG

With royal punctuality the sovereign lady and her suite rolled up in their carriages, drove round the arena in state, and dismounted at the entrance to the box. The august company included, besides her Majesty, their Royal Highnesses Prince and Princess Henry of Battenberg, the Marquis of Lorne, the Dowager Duchess of Athole and the Hon. Ethel Cadogan, Sir Henry and Lady Ponsonby, General Lynedoch Gardiner, Colonel Sir Henry Ewart, Lord Ronald Gower and a collection of uniformed celebrities and brilliantly attired fair ladies who formed a veritable parterre of living flowers around the temporary throne[52]. During our introduction a very notable incident occurred, sufficient to send the blood surging through every American's veins at Niagara speed. As usual in our entertainment, the American flag, carried by a graceful, well-mounted horseman, was introduced, with the statement that it was "an emblem of peace and friendship to all the world." As the standard-bearer waved the proud emblem above his head, Her Majesty rose from her seat and bowed deeply and impressively towards the banner. The whole court party rose, the ladies bowed, the generals present saluted, and the English noblemen took off their hats.

Then—we couldn't help it—but there arose such a

17. Saluting Her Majesty, Queen Victoria.

genuine heart-stirring American yell from our company as seemed to shake the sky. It was a great event. For the first time in history, since the Declaration of Independence, a sovereign of Great Britain had saluted the star spangled banner, and that banner was carried by a member of Buffalo Bill's Wild West! All present were constrained to feel that here was an outward and visible sign of the extinction of that mutual prejudice, sometimes almost amounting to race hatred, that has severed the two nations from the times of Washington and George the Third to the present day. We felt that the hatchet was buried at last and the Wild West had been at the funeral.

PRESENTED TO THE QUEEN

Under the stimulus of the Queen's presence, the performance was admirably given. The whole company seemed infected with a determination to excel themselves. Personally I missed not a single shot; the young ladies excelled themselves in the same line; the charges on the Indians were delivered with a terrific *vim*; and the very bucking horses seemed to buck like steam-engines under the influence of that half minute of excitement. But perhaps this last may have been fancy. Better than all, the Queen not only abandoned her original intention of remaining to see only the first acts, but saw the whole thing through, and wound up with a "command" that Buffalo Bill should be presented to her. Her compliments, deliberate and unmeasured, modesty forbids me to repeat.

A kindly little lady, not five feet in height, but every inch a gracious queen. I had the pleasure of presenting Miss Lilian Smith, the mechanism of whose Winchester repeater was explained to Her Majesty, who takes a remarkable interest in fire-arms. Young California spoke up gracefully and like a little woman. Then Nate Salsbury was commanded to the presence and introduced, and took his blushing honors with all the grace of the polished American gentleman he is. Next came Red Shirt, gorgeous in his war-paint and most splendiferous feather trappings. His proud bearing seemed to fetch the royal party immensely, and when he quietly declared that "he had come a long way to see Her Majesty, and felt glad," and strolled abruptly away with dignity spread all over him three inches thick, the Queen smiled appreciatively, as who should say, "I know a real Duke when I see him." Finally two squaws were summoned, and came racing across the arena, their little brown papooses slung behind them. Upon these royalty, unbending, "rained gracious influence." The papooses were handed up for inspection, and behaved themselves nicely while Her Majesty petted them. And so the Queen's visit came to an end, with a last command, expressed through Sir Henry Ponsonby, that a record of all she had seen should be sent on to Windsor. A great occasion, of which the mental photograph will long remain with me.

STATESMEN AT THE WILD WEST

Of the statesmen and men otherwise eminent who visited the Wild West in these bright summer days—it was a wonderful summer for England—a partial list will be found elsewhere. One of the earliest was John Bright, to whose honored name no Englishman ever thinks of tacking the "Mister."[53] The People's Tribune met with an unfortunate accident on entering the show, reminding one of William the Conqueror's when he made that awkward stumble on Hasting's beach, to the dismay of his followers, who thought it a bad omen, and rose exclaiming: "Lo, here have I already seized two handfuls of this English earth; let us go on, my bully boys, and rope in the remainder." That was distinctly clever. John Bright tripped over the rubber mat at my tent portal, and arose, grasping, not the English earth, but the end of his nose, which was bleeding. I was truly distressed at this awkward fall occurring to the venerated leader, and made him as comfortable as possible in my tent until he had got over the shock. Major Burke stood by with much heroism and a bottle of eau-de-cologne and bathed the afflicted spot until the illustrious patient felt all right and able to go to his seat. The news of the accident had spread through the auditorium, and when the "old man eloquent" made his appearance in his box, smiling and quite chipper again, the packed audience gave him three mighty cheers that made him laugh some more.

Lord Randolph Churchill had heard of the incident, and it was quite amusing to see him look at that mat next time he came to the show, gather his muscles together, and deliberately leap over it. A born humorist is his lordship, affectionately dubbed "Little Randy" by the conservative democracy, principally because *Mr. Punch*[54] delights in depicting him as a whipper-snapper. After all he is not a short man, either in stature or in intellectual "change." He is a right smart politician and one of the pleasantest of the many pleasant English gentlemen it has been my good fortune to meet.

A RIB-ROAST BREAKFAST, A LA INDIAN, TO GEN. CAMERON

While receiving generous attention from the most prominent people of England, I was by no means neglected by my own countrymen, many of whom were frequent visitors to the Wild West Show and who otherwise added, by their presence and influence, much to the popularity of the show and myself as well. Hon. James G. Blaine, accompanied by his family, spent several hours with me in my tent and was a frequent visitor to the show. So, also, was Hon. Joseph Pulitzer, Chauncy M. De Pew, Lawrence Jerome, Murat Halstead, General Hawley, Simon Cameron, and many other distinguished Americans.[55] So many prominent Americans of my acquaintance were in London at the time, that Mr. Salsbury and I decided to give several of our countrymen a novel entertainment that would serve the double purpose of regaling their appetites while affording an illustration of the wild habits of many Indian tribes. In pursuance of our resolve we invited Gen. Simon Cameron[56] as the specially honored guest of the occasion, and about one hundred other Americans, including in the list all of those named above, to a Rib-roast Breakfast, which was to be prepared by the Indians after the manner of their cooking when in their native habitat.

At nine o'clock in the morning all the invited guests responded to the summons and came to our large dining tent that was gorgeously festooned and decorated for the occasion. Before the tent a fire had been made, around which grouped a number of Indian cooks. A hole had been dug in the ground and in this a great bed of coals was now made, over which was set a wooden tripod from which was suspended several ribs of beef. An Indian noted for his skill as a rib-roaster attended to the cooking by gently moving the meat over the hot coals for nearly half an hour, when it was removed to the quarters and there jointed ready to be served. The guests were much interested in the process of cooking and were equally anxious to sample the product of Indian culinary art. Several long tables, *al a* barbecue style, were set upon which the *menu* was spread consisting of ribs of beef, Indian style, grub-stakes, salmon, roast beef, roast mutton, ham, tongue, stewed chicken, lobster salad, American hominy and milk, corn, potatoes, cocoanut pie, apple pie, Wild West pudding, American pop corn and peanuts.

The whole of the Indian tribes in camp breakfasted with the visitors, squatting on straw at the end of the long dining tent. Each "brave" had a sharp white stake in front of him, on which he impaled his portion of rib when not gnawing it from his fingers. Some dozen ribs were cooked and eaten in this primitive fashion, civilized and savage methods of eating confronting each other. The thoroughly typical breakfast over, excellent speeches, chiefly of a humorous nature, were made by the honored guest, Gen. Cameron, and Chauncy M. De Pew, Mr. Lawrence Jerome, Murat Halsted, General Joe. Hawley,

18. The Indian Dance Before My Guests.

Justin McCarthy, M. P., Red Shirt, Mr. Salsbury and myself. After the speeches an Indian dance was given, and the guests finally withdrew sometime after noon, while a majority availed themselves of an invitation to witness the Wild West entertainment.

THE PRINCE OF WALES AND HIS ROYAL FLUSH

Business continued to boom splendidly, and yet another excitement was in store for us. There came to Earl's Court, carried by a royal equerry, a further command from her Majesty conveying the royal pleasure that on the 20th of June a special morning exhibition of the Wild West should be given to the kingly and princely guests of Queen Victoria on the occasion of her Jubilee. This was the third entertainment given to royalty in private, and surely never before since the world commenced has such a gathering honored a public entertainment. Cæsar and his captive monarchs, the Field of the Cloth of Gold[57]—nothing in history can compare with that gathering of the mighty ones of the earth which honored our entertainment. The Queen was to treat them to a display of quite another kind in Westminster Abbey the following day; but the Wild West was beforehand with her Majesty as will be seen. I was getting fairly hardened to royalty by this time; I had exhibited before it; I had met it at private parties and at club-houses; and I had seen it in its best aspects, honoring and honored by communion with that other royalty of brains which holds high court in England as everywhere. But this was to be a knock-down in the royalty line—a regular wholesale consignment—a pack of cards

19. Giving Royalty a Spin during an Attack by Indians.

all pictures and waited on by the brightest, best and bravest and most beautiful that all Europe and a good part of Asia could produce. The gathering of personages consisted of the King of Denmark, the King of Saxony, the King and Queen of the Belgians, and the King of Greece, the Crown Prince of Austria, the Prince and Princess of Saxe-Meiningen, the Crown Prince and Princess of Germany, the Crown Prince of Sweden and Norway, the Princess Victoria of Prussia, the Duke of Sparta, the Grand Duke Michael of Russia, Prince George of Greece, Prince Louis of Baden and last, but not least, the Prince and Princess of Wales with their family, besides a great host of lords and ladies innumerable.

Our good old Deadwood coach, "baptized in fire and blood" so repeatedly on the plains, had the honor of carrying on its time-honored timbers four kings and the Prince of Wales that day, during the attack of the redskins. Said His Royal Highness to me, when the show was over:

"Colonel, you never held four kings like these before."

"I've held four kings," said I, "but four kings and the Prince of Wales makes a royal flush, such as no man ever held before."

I suppose my old poker-playing experiences were instinctively in the ascendant and prompted the retort. The Prince took it, and went off with that hair-trigger laugh of his that is so well known to his intimates. To their European majesties the joke was somewhat recondite, and I almost pitied the Prince as he tried to explain it in three languages to his wondering but obtuse auditors. They don't play poker yet at the continental courts, and come to think of it, the game *does* want a deal of learning before you get the hang of it properly. I hope their majesties enjoyed that ride, but the Indians put in their shooting with a lot of energy, and somehow the crowned heads appeared to be glad when it was over.

THE PRINCE PRESENTS ME WITH A DIAMOND PIN

The appended letter of thanks from Marlborough House after this interesting gathering will probably be of as much interest to my readers as it was to myself:

> Marlborough House,
> Pall Mall, S.W.
>
> Dear Sir: —Lieut.-General Sir Dighton Probyn, Comptroller and Treasurer of the Prince of Wales's household, presents his compliments to Colonel Cody and is directed by his Royal Highness to forward him the accompanying pin as a souvenir of the performance of the Wild West, which Colonel Cody gave before the Prince and Princess of Wales, the Kings of Denmark, Belgium, Greece and Saxony and other royal guests on Monday last, to all of whom, the Prince desires Sir Dighton Probyn to say, the entertainment gave great satisfaction.
>
> London, June 22d, 1887

A further souvenir, which I shall ever highly prize, took the form of the pin already referred to—the Prince of Wales's feathers worked in diamonds, with the motto "Ich dien" ("I serve") beneath. The story of how this crest and motto were wrested from the King of Bohemia at Cressy by the Black Prince, son of Edward III., of England, will, perhaps, be familiar to my youthful readers.[58]

20. Pin Presented Me by the Prince of Wales.

THE PRINCESS RIDES IN THE DEADWOOD COACH

The Prince and Princess and their sons and daughters were frequent visitors during our stay in London. On one occasion her Royal Highness determined to try the novel sensation of a ride in the old stage, and sent me an intimation of her desire. I went to the royal box to mention the exact time at which the coach would start, and found that her royal lord and master had weighty objections to any such proceeding. He may not have liked it over well himself, and seemed a little nervous. But "when a lady will, she will, and there's an end on't," as the old proverb says, and so the gentle Alexandra was booked for inside passage, and took it smilingly. Her spouse seemed much relieved when we delivered her up safe and sound after her exciting expedition; for herself she seemed highly delighted, and thanked me effusively for the novel pleasure she had experienced.

The Princess's liking for the entertainment seemed to grow upon acquaintance. I received one day a startling intimation to the effect that the Princess would that evening visit the show *incognita*. For a royal lady whose face is as well known in London as that of Big Ben at Westminster this seemed considerably cool. Our manager, whose duty it was to receive her, declared himself in a "middling tight fix." The hour came, and with it the willful lady, and the Major assisted her from her private carriage into the lobby.

"Your Royal Highness will not desire to use your own box, perhaps?" he said.

"No, sir; your band will play the national anthem, and then I am in plain view, you see, discovered. Is it not?"

This was charmingly said, in her pretty unidiomatic English, but the gallant manager rubbed his chin.

"Has your Royal Highness a desire for any particular position?" he asked.

"Certainly, yes. Put me immediately amongst the people. I like the people."

Then the manager "struck a bright idea." It was an off-night for the newspaper men, and the commodious press box was sacred from intrusion. Into the press box accordingly he ushered the royal lady and her attendant. The performance had hardly commenced when—horror of horrors!—in came a triplet of hardy press men and a lady. To the manager and myself alone of all our company was the secret of the Princess's visit known. Consequently the attendants ushered the new-comers into their usual seats without question and closed the door behind them.

Presently to the manager "dancing on thorns," came one of the newspaper boys: "Say, partner, will you mind saying who are our companions? I really never saw such a likeness in all my life to—"

"I know what you are going to say," said the manager; "the resemblance really *is* rather striking. But come along; I'll introduce you."

The thing had to be bluffed out somehow; and in due course the press men were formally introduced to "Colonel and Mrs. Jones, friends of mine from Texas," by the imperturbable manager, who believes in taking the bull by the horns.

The Princess took the joke with becoming gravity, although her companion seemed horribly disturbed. She confessed afterwards that it was one of the pleasantest and funniest evenings she had ever spent in her life. As to the manager he was in a cold perspiration until he had steered his onerous charge through the departing crowd of sight-seers and seen her comfortably seated in her carriage. His attempt at a murmured apology was cut short by a silvery laugh, as the Princess remarked the "evening has been most enjoyable and the adventure one grand success," and so, as the Frenchmen say, "the incident closed itself."

CLOSE OF THE LONDON SEASON

And so amidst innumerable social junketings, feastings, and courtly functions which now seem like the glistening pageant of a fairy dream thrown suddenly athwart the memories of my war-like, rough-and-tumble earlier career, our London experiences drew to a successful close. We had been making "barrels of money;" but it had been hard work for all hands, doubly and trebly hard for me, living the life of a hard-working member of the company; responsible master of our singularly complicated gathering of wild spirits from the several regions of half-civilized America, north, west, and south, and greatest if pleasantest toil of all, the feted guest of all that was rich and frivolous, royal and talented, great and Bohemian in that mighty mixed congeries of many-shaded humanity, London society. I wonder as I write how much of me is flesh and blood, and how much steel and leather, that I should have endured the strain without breaking down. A man wants hardening for a life on the plains; but he wants to be tanned and tempered, hammered and welded into adamant to stand the tension of such a life as mine during that summer season. We had all the elements of success, a continuity of delightful weather, unknown in England for thirty years before our coming; an appreciative community, the help of hundreds of kind friends in the press and in society, to whom my gratitude is and ever will be inexpressible; and lastly, a really first-rate entertainment that awoke a strongly sympathetic response in the generous public sentiment of the British nation. With one more extract I conclude this eventful epoch of our history. It is from the "Thunderer" of Printing-house square; the great *Times* itself, and will serve to fitly round off my story of our magnificent reception in the metropolis of Britain, with its 100 square miles of bricks and mortar, and its population of 5,000,000 souls (asserted). It was printed on Nov. 1, the day after our final triumphant performance:

> The Wild West Exhibition, which has attracted all the town to West Brompton for the last few months, was brought yesterday to an appropriate and dignified close. A meeting of representative Englishmen and Americans was held, under the presidency of Lord Lorne, in support of the movement for establishing a Court of Arbitration for the settlement of disputes between this country and the United States. At first sight it might seem to be a far cry from the Wild West to an International Court. Yet the connection is not really very remote. Exhibitions of American products and of a few scenes from the wilder phases of American life certainly tend in some degree at least to bring America nearer to England. They are partly cause and partly effect. They are the effect of increased and increasing intercourse between the two countries, and they tend to promote a still more intimate understanding. The two things, the Exhibition and the Wild West Show, have supplemented each other. Those who went to

be amused often stayed to be instructed. It must be acknowledged that the show was the attraction which made the fortune of the Exhibition. Without Colonel Cody, his cowboys, and his Indians, it is conceivable that the Exhibition might have reproduced the Wild West in one feature at any rate—namely, its solitude—with rare fidelity. But the Wild West was irresistible. Colonel Cody, much to the astonishment of some of his more superfine compatriots, suddenly found himself the hero of the London season. Notwithstanding his daily engagements and his punctual fulfillment of them, he found time to go everywhere, to see everything, and to be seen by all the world. All London contributed to his triumph, and now the close of his show is selected as the occasion for promoting a great international movement with Mr. Bright, Lord Granville, Lord Wolseley, and Lord Lorne for its sponsors. Colonel Cody can achieve no greater triumph than this, even if he someday realizes the design attributed to him of running the Wild West Show within the classic precincts of the Colosseum at Rome.

To which last suggestion, all I have to reply is that if the Colosseum at Rome possessed the requisite accommodation for an enterprise of the magnitude of the Wild West more unlikely things might well happen than a visit by our combination to the city of the Seven Hills. Columbus was a Genoese, and there would be no irreverence to antiquity in presenting his Italian fellow-countrymen with a few phases in the history of that gigantic New World which he was the first to bring to the knowledge of the old.

OUR TOUR IN "THE PROVINCES"

A brief but successful occupancy of the Aston Lower Grounds, Birmingham, followed almost immediately upon our London triumphs. Birmingham, the headquarters of the British gun-making industry, the fancy metal trades and of innumerable branches of the lighter hardware crafts, together with its numerous surrounding towns responded nobly to our invitation. The news of our reception in London had gone before us, and we met with a prodigious welcome from the screw-makers, the teapot turners and the manufacturers of artificial jewelry and "Brummagem goods"[59] in general. But with the drifting season there were signs that the weather was breaking. It was manifest that the Wild West must get under cover in winter quarters, and a mightier center than Birmingham was extending its arms to us farther north.

Manchester, with its surrounding network of a hundred smaller but yet important towns—"Cottonopolis," as it is endearingly called by its denizens—was issuing pressing invitations. This powerful district resembles nothing so much as a still greater London, split and separated by the explosion of a bombshell. A population of some six million toilers in mine and mill, divided into communities of from 10,000 to 100,000 or so, yet linked to the great center by a spider's web of railways—such was the object of our next and perhaps most gigantic effort of all.

A VISIT TO ITALY

During the period of preparation for opening the Wild West exhibition in Manchester, I took advantage of the spare time that was offered, and with my daughter, Arta, spent a well-earned vacation of two weeks in Italy. I say well-earned because from the day of opening our show in London until the close of our engagement in that city I had not missed a single one of the three hundred performances given, notwithstanding the unexampled social courtesies that I was compelled to observe, which kept me occupied nearly eighteen hours out of every twenty-four. At one time it had been the ambition of Mr. Salsbury and myself to give a Wild West exhibition in the ancient Colosseum of Rome, but an examination of the ruins and surroundings speedily convinced me that to make the attempt would be a vaulting ambition overleaping itself, and the idea was abandoned. I made a rather hasty tour of the more important cities of Italy, but can hardly admit that the trip was an enjoyable one on account of a constant realization of the necessity of my presence with the show, and the hurried manner in which I was compelled to make my visit. Accordingly, I returned to Manchester and helped prepare for opening the winter season there.

The English winter, if not subject to such intense frosts

and other rigors as are known to the American climate, is yet an extremely trying season. Variety, it is said, is charming, but he must be an optimist indeed, who can be charmed with the mixture of weather which favored us during our stay in the great northern center. Rain, fog, frost, drizzle, snow and searching east wind followed each other in fantastic succession, not one of them staying long enough to assert itself as the prevalent weather, but giving us a very choice assortment of samples. We had prepared for this state of things, however. The Manchester race-course, which, by the way, is situated in the adjoining borough of Salford, on the banks of the inky ditch known as the Irwell, is made on a magnificent stretch of green sward easily accessible from all parts of the district. At the race meetings which occur several times in the course of each year, it is not uncommon for 80,000 or 100,000 persons to assemble on this tract of land. Here, then, I decided to pitch our tents and go into winter quarters. In the short space of two months the largest theater ever seen in the world was erected by an enterprising firm of Manchester builders, together with a commodious building attached to it for the accommodation of the troop, whose tents and tepees were erected under its shelter, the whole of the structures being comfortably heated by steam and illuminated by the electric light. One great advantage of the race-course was the large and splendidly appointed range of stables, generally used for the accommodation of the horses of the English turf, which were placed at our disposal. The buildings in which Ormonde, Ben. d'Or, Robert the Devil, and a thousand other world-famed equine wonders had taken their rest and refreshment, were now appropriated to the comfort of our bronchos, mustangs and other four-footed coadjutors. Of the vast theater itself, and the novel style of entertainment which I had the pleasure of introducing to the hard-working millions and the cotton and iron princes of the North of England, no more vivid picture can be presented than that drawn by the reporter of the *Sunday Chronicle*, a paper of enormous influence in the wide area whose people we intended to attract. I may premise that the splendid scenery used upon our mammoth stage was from the brush of Mr. Matt. Morgan, an English artist whose name is familiar to Americans.[60] The scenes, which cost us $40,000, were from nature, and enabled us to combine the painted full effects of a gigantic stage display with the free movement of our 250 horsemen upon the open plain. Says the reporter:

Description of the Show

A vast amphitheater, shaped somewhat like a horseshoe magnet, with giant proscenium stretched across its poles; an enormous stage, constructed without flooring, the scenery and set pieces of which are let down upon the bare earth; a drama, dealing with a period of five hundred years, in which nearly three hundred men and women, and as many horses, buffaloes, and other four-footed creatures take part, performed in great measure immediately under the eyes of the spectators, on a huge plain level with the stage and drifting into a perspective upon it—such is a general description of the performance which was given for the first time yesterday afternoon by Colonel Cody and his magnificent troupe. The theater, brilliantly lighted and well warmed throughout, is like nothing else ever constructed in this country. The seats, accommodating nearly ten thousand persons, are ranged in tiers, from the pew-like private boxes in front to a height of forty feet or so; and the distance from the extreme end of the auditorium to the back of the stage is so great that a horseman galloping across the whole area diminishes by natural perspective until the spectator is fairly cheated into the idea that the journey is to be prolonged until the rider vanishes in the pictured horizon. The illusion, indeed, is so well managed and complete, the boundless plains and swelling prairies are so vividly counterfeited, that it is difficult to resist the belief that we are really gazing over an immense expanse of country from some hillside in the far West. The pictures, from the brush of the talented Matt. Morgan, are singularly beautiful in themselves, and it only needs the constantly varying groups of living men and animals in front of them to complete the charm.

In arranging the latest development of their exhibition, Messrs. Cody and Salsbury have undertaken no trifling task. Besides the displays of horsemanship and feats of shooting with which the notices of their doings in London have familiarized the public, they have determined to present the story of the development of the American Continent from primeval times until the present day. It is a play without a plot and without dialogue, unless the clever and humorous lecture of Mr. Frank Richmond, the "orator" of the establishment, can be called such. This gentleman occupies a lofty pulpit to the left of the proscenium, and it says much for the acoustic properties of the gigantic building that his voice can be heard so distinctly as it is. The drama, however, has no lack of coherence, and the interest of the spectators is unflaggingly sustained throughout the long succession of exciting scenes from the introduction to the close.

By the plan adopted the entertainment is divided into "episodes," of which the first, after the preliminary of a general personal introduction of the troupe, is the Forest Primeval, in which

> The murmuring pines and the hemlocks
> Bearded with moss, and in garments green,
> Indistinct in the twilight,
> Stand like Druids of old.

It is midnight, and wild animals lie scattered about in their lairs. With the opening dawn we make the acquaintance of the Red Indian as he used to be before the white man crowded him out of his possessions. At sunrise—a beautifully stage-managed effect—we have the meeting of two Indian tribes, who execute a friendly dance to a quaint barbaric measure. Then comes a courier with notice of the approach of a hostile tribe intent upon massacre and the collection of scalps. The attack is delivered with terrific vigor, and the battle that ensues is an unequalled picture of savage warfare.

The Second Episode deals with the landing of the Pilgrim Fathers from the Mayflower on Plymouth Rock, with which the era of civilization is held to commence. Here, again, the scenery is remarkably fine, and the characters in the tableau are characteristically dressed in the short capes, steeple-crowned hats, and sad-colored Puritan raiment of religious England in their day. From this, amidst

21. Cowboy Lassoing an Indian.

appropriate music from Mr. Sweeny's Cowboy Band, the scene changes to Episode No. 3, the rescue from death of that heroic bearer of an honored name, John Smith, by that beauteous Indian princess, Pocahontas. Now ensues a most interesting delineation of Indian manners and customs, from the wedding to the war dance, by the whole of the Indian forces, under the command of Red Shirt himself.

With the Fourth Episode we reach more stirring scenes. The picture, composed of innumerable front sets and a most lovely background, by Matt Morgan, represents the prairie, with a drinking pool, or "lick," in the foreground, to which the wild buffaloes come to slake their thirst. In pursuit of the great game comes Buffalo Bill himself, on his famous horse, Old Charlie, who has covered one hundred miles in less than ten hours, conducting an emigrant train of white folks, with wagons, horsemen, women, and children, and all the accessories of a march across the wilderness. In the gathering twilight they camp around the pool, the fires are lit, and a clever performance of the "Virginia horseback reel" takes place. Subsequently, with the gathering darkness, the camp sinks into slumber, and for awhile all is still. Then comes a piece of stage managing, which more nearly approaches the terrible than anything ever yet attempted in this country. A red streak upon the horizon gives warning that some unwonted danger is approaching the sleeping folks; the glow broadens and deepens, and seems to creep gradually over the pictured miles of open country, until the slumbering people are roused with the appalling intelligence that the prairie is on fire. The conflagration approaches nearer and nearer, until the whole landscape appears one lurid mass of incandescence, and the roaring flames leap down upon the foreground with wild fury, threatening all concerned with a horrible death. The men endeavor to stamp out the conflagration with their rugs and blankets, and in the midst of the horror there swoops upon them a maddened rush of wild animals, flying from the fire, and a "stampede" ensues in all its terrors. This scene, which reflects the highest credit upon the stage management, is one of the grandest ever placed before the public, and fairly baffles description.

Next ensues some cowboy and Mexican vaquero business with bucking horses, throwing the lasso, in which that handsome cavalier and King of the Cowboys, Buck Taylor, figures conspicuously; and we get some extraordinary feats in shooting by Johnny Baker, the Cowboy Kid, all of which is very novel and amusing. And so we arrive at the Fifth Episode, the scene of which is a cattle ranch in the Wild West, with a real log hut and all appropriate surroundings. The settlers, after an interesting representation of camp life in the wilds, are attacked by Indians, and a fierce battle ensues, which is waged with varying fortunes until it ends in the rescue of the besieged party by a band of whites, and the flight of the Redskins. An interlude is occupied by some fancy rifle shooting by Miss Lillian Smith, "the California girl," and then we come to another grand historical tableau in the Sixth Episode, wherein is set out the routine of a military camp on the frontier. The unfortunate General Custer, occupying with his regiment a stockade or log fort, receives intimation of the discovery of a camp of hostile Indians by his scouts. "Boots and saddle" is sounded, and the troops move off to the second scene, which is the camp of Sitting Bull and his braves on the Little Big Horn river. The ambush and subsequent massacre of the whole of the gallant band of white men is presented with vivid realism, and the battle-field by night, which closes the episode, develops in its full horrors what has been fitly called "the reddest page of savage history."

A brilliant display of shooting on foot and on horseback by Buffalo Bill himself is now given in the arena, and the magical promptitude with which glass balls and other small objects are shattered before his never-erring aim while riding at full speed must be seen to be believed. In this remarkable exhibition, as in the other shooting performances, the iron fireproof curtain is made to do duty

22. Lassoing Horses in the Wild West Show.

as a background or target, and the whole performance may be warranted to take the conceit out of any ordinary marksman. It is nothing less than marvellous.

The Seventh Episode, which marks a still later period of frontier life, is perhaps the most exciting and picturesque of the whole entertainment. The first scene is a mining camp, "Deadwood City," in the Black Hills, with the "Wild West Tavern" in the foreground, and we are treated *seriatim*[61] to the incidents of a miners' holiday, with a shooting match, the arrival of the pony express, and a frontier duel, with its characteristic ending of "another man for breakfast." Then comes the departure of the Deadwood Coach, and the scene changes to a "canyon" or rocky pass in the hills. The Deadwood Coach with its freight of passengers, guards and "shotgun messengers," is fallen upon in the canyon by Indians, and a stubborn battle occurs, in which the passengers are likely to succumb, when they are rescued by the sudden appearance of Buffalo Bill and his Cowboy cavalry.

It will be seen that there is no lack of exciting business in all this, and the consumption of gunpowder is enormous. The members of the company go at their work with appalling zest, and their picturesque mingling of spirited horses, quaint costumes and warlike impedimenta, in all the wild confusion of a frontier melee, is brilliantly effective. In the third scene of this episode we return to the mountain village, in which the climax of scenic effect is reached by the production of a genuine cyclone. Powerful wind-making machinery has been put down for this purpose, and a blast is delivered upon the stage strong enough to rend the log cabins to pieces, and scatter their fragments, together with wagons, camp furniture, and even human beings from one side of the stage to the other. The howling of the tornado and the disastrous effect of its resistless current are realistically presented. How it is done is, of course, a stage secret, but there is no gainsaying the magnificent completeness with which the hurricane gets in its work and reduces the camp of the little mining community to chaos. This brings the performance to an effective close.

THE CROWD AT OUR OPENING PERFORMANCE

As a "send-off" to the new departure we had invited the whole of the beauty, rank and fashion of Manchester and the surrounding towns to a gratis performance of this programme two days before our opening date. The mayors, town councils, corporation officials, prominent merchants and manufacturers, bishops and clergy of all denominations, and an able-bodied horde of pressmen came down in their thousands. From Liverpool across country through Leeds and York to Hull and Newcastle, and from Carlisle as far south as Birmingham, everybody of consequence was present, and the immense building was filled to its utmost capacity. The notice above quoted will show that all had reason to be pleased, and the story they had to tell of the marvellous things to be witnessed at the Wild West spread with lightning rapidity through every town from which they had gathered together. The consequence was that from our opening day it was often difficult to cope with the throngs who presented themselves at afternoon and evening performances, alike to feast their eyes upon the dangers and the glories of America's development. Despite the dreary winter weather, or perhaps because of it, the well-lighted, well-warmed "Temple of Buffalo Bill and Thespis,"[62] as somebody called it, was the constant resort of pleasure-seeking throngs.

Amongst other demands upon our seating space came scores of requisitions from the heads of schools and charitable institutions, which are thickly scattered through the mining, weaving and spinning towns of Bolton, Bury, Rochdale, Oldham, Stalybridge and a hundred more, as well as those in Manchester and Salford. "What is the lowest price at which you can allow us to give our little waifs a treat?" was the burden of I don't know how many letters. My invariable reply was "Let us know your numbers and come on Wednesday afternoon, which is the only time when we are not over-crowded, and we will fix you up for nothing at all, if we have to turn money away for you." I lay claim to no credit for generosity in this particular, for each invitation of the kind increased our popularity to a surprising extent, and it was only a further example of the good policy of "casting your bread upon the waters." Amongst these juvenile visitors were the 100 inmates of Chetham's College, a Manchester charitable institution dating back to the times of Henry VI., the boys of which are still quartered in the fine old Gothic building erected during the Wars of the Roses, over a hundred years before Columbus turned his vessel's prow to the westward and steered for nowhere in particular, to the great horror of the Old World navigators of his time.

During our stay in Cottonopolis I found the same ungrudging and overwhelming social hospitality that had tried my physical powers so severely in the capital. "Thrones, powers, dominions," and dynastic royalty are of course conspicuous by their absence from this vast manufacturing, money-making heart of Northern activity. But that sublimer royalty of commerce, of invention, of fire and steel, of ever-flying shuttle and spindle here holds high state, and its entertainments are princely in scope and hearty in their hospitality. They have a pride of their own, too, these coal and cotton lords and self-made millionaires. The man himself and the great things he has done for humanity are held in more esteem than long descent or the glamors of inherited wealth. I found here, in fact, a closer resemblance to the natural dignity of the American citizen than I had experienced elsewhere in England. My invitation list would occupy more space than I can afford.

PRESENTED WITH A RIFLE

One event, amongst my endeavors to make some return for this unbounded stream of hospitality, caused a considerable sensation in the district, from its novelty. It had been determined by the artistic, dramatic, and literary gentlemen of Manchester to make me a public presentation of a magnificent rifle, decked in flowers and gaily adorned with ribbons, and the event having got wind in London, the *elite* of the metropolitan *literati*, headed by Sir Somers Vine[63] and including representatives of all the great American journals, secured a special train and ran up to Manchester, some hundred strong, to grace the ceremony with their presence. The happy thought struck me of inviting the whole crowd of local celebrities and London visitors to what for them would be an entirely original lay-out. This was a camp dinner, with fried oysters, Boston pork and beans, Maryland chicken, and other American dishes, and a real Indian "rib-roast" as the *piece de resistance*.

The presentation, which took place in the arena, being over, the banquet was held in the race-course pavilion. The Mayor of Salford and a number of civic dignitaries from both Manchester and the neighboring borough graced the table with their presence; United States Consul Moffat of London honored me with his company and

Consul Hale of Manchester—a gentleman held in high and well deserved respect by the whole of the rich and powerful community amongst whom he resides and labors—made the speech of the evening. Nate Salsbury, as the vice-chairman, simply excelled himself; and the comments of the English guests upon the novel and to them outlandish fare they were consuming were highly amusing to us of the American party. I have reason to believe that the corn-cake, hominy, and other American fixings, were a complete revelation to them. The rib-roast, served in tin platters and eaten in the fingers, without knives or forks, was a source of huge wonderment. I reckon that Englishmen never toasted the American flag more heartily, and for a week afterwards the press of the country was dilating on the strange and savage doings at the Wild West camp. A newspaper genius of Manchester, who seems to have studied his Longfellow[64] to some purpose, gushed into blank verse with the following epic, entitled:

The Rib-Roast Of Pa-He-Haska.[65]

Mr. Editor.—
Should you ask me whence this poem,
Whence this yarn of tangled meaning,
With its odor of Havana,
And its marks of Mumm's best vintage
Staining every side of copy,
Staining text and staining margin—
I should answer, I should tell you:
From the festive board of William,
From the feast of Pa-he-haska,
Long haired lord of many cowboys—

Buffalo Bill, the mighty hunter
From across the Gitche-Gumee
("Herring-pond" is what *we* call it).
When he fed the London Pressmen
On the Muskoday, the meadow
On the Manchester big Racecourse.
****

In the lodges of the Turfites,
There we gathered in the evening,
In the gloaming, O my darling!
When the *matinee* was over.

Many chieftains came from London,
Many from the heap big village,
Pioneered by stout Tom Burnside,
With his waist of grand dimensions—
Equatorial enlargement—
On some cheeks the Pressman's totem
Oza-wa-beek, or the brass-mark,
Glowed, as round the board they gathered,
While the Manchester contingent,
Merry drivers of the goose-quill—
Of the quills of Wa-be-wawa—
Mingled with their Cockney brothers
Mingled, too, with many Yankees
From across the Gitche-Gumee—
Uncle Sam's ink-slinging nephews.

If but distantly related
Yet in universal kinship
Held by bonds of gratis luncheon.
****

At the top end of the table
Sat the noble Pa-he-haska—
Buffalo Bill in all his glory!
Mighty Moffat, London Consul
And the puissant Mayor of Salford,
Sachem of the model borough,
With his elders grave in council
(Not too grave when flows the grape-juice),
Flanked the chieftain on his right hand,
Fed like men well used to camp life,
Used to all a Hunter's manners!

On his left was Hale, the Consul,
From his eagle eyes out flashing
Uncle Sam's reflected glory!
In the vice-chair sat Nathaniel—
"Nate" they call him in the programmes,
Star-tongued Salsbury, William's partner,
Wary wielder of straight language.

Stalwart John of Arizona—
Major Burke, sun-browned and war scarred,
Like Ke-neu, the great war-eagle
Hovered round about the table—
Kept the laughing wine-cup flowing.
Unk-ta-hee, the god of water
Didn't have a look-in at us!

And the store of food outlandish
Disappeared before the Pressmen:
Dish by dish in swift destruction
Melted in the purple distance.

Bean soup first and then fried oysters;
Ribs of Pez-he-kee, the bison,
Served on plates of tin and garnished
With the sweet corn, the Mon-da-min—
Eaten in true savage fashion;
Knife and fork alike forbidden—
Gnaw the bone and suck your fingers,
That's the way to cop the flavor—
Of the noble redskin's rib-roast.

Pork and beans, that's Boston's glory,
Buck wheat cakes and thick molasses
Hominy and piccalilli,
Went their way to bright Po-ne-mah
To the Land of the Hereafter.

All the while a rhythmic plashing—
Mu-way-aush-ka, sound of sea waves!—
Pop of corks, and clink of glasses,
Told the dark-eyed Pa-he-haska—
Told the stalwart Colonel Cody
That his guests were not neglectful:
They could stand it long as he could,
Possibly might stand it longer!
****
Shall I tell you of the speeches,
Of the pow-wow and palaver?
How the Mayor pledg'd Buffalo William,
How the Consul praised his valor,
Told how in the fight he'd met him,
On the field of death—of Pau-guk?
How Nate Salsbury's health, twice toasted,

Made him feel done brown on both sides.
How Red Shirt, the fighting chieftain,
Spoke in paragraphic Choctaw,
Telling us, as 'twas translated,
That he loved his pale-face brothers
Better than he loved his dinner,
And would meet us up in heaven—
In the Land of bright Po-ne-mah?—
(Red Shirt doesn't seem to know us,
Has not seen us paint the town red!)—
How the Pressmen all responded
"Ugh! "which means in English "Rather!"
How we pledged the noble chieftain
Till we saw two Red Shirts looming—
Looming through the pale Puk-wana—
Through the clouds of much tobacco?

****

No; I'll spare my paleface kinsmen
All the pain of that recital,
Just as I'd not rather dwell on
Certain subsequent proceedings;
Or our feelings in the morning.
When the med'cine men, the Me-das,
Gave us physic antibilious
So that we might keep our end up,
Keep our end up, and look sober.

****

Gone are all those London persons,
Swept they southward, wild and boozy,
Like the cloud-wrack of a tempest,
Like the withered leaves of autumn

Scattered by Wild West tornado;
And their Shaw-shaws, their big swallows,
Now mop up the damp in Fleet-street,
Mop up all superfluous moisture.

Buffalo William still is with us,
So's Buck Taylor, so is Red Shirt,
And the Major's convalescing
Bet your life, he's still on deck here!
Still the Wild West Show is booming,
Booming just as it deserves to,
If I say the thing that is not,
Call me Ya-goo, call me liar!

But whene'er that feed's repeated,
Call me Early, Major darling,
Call me not too late for dinner!

ENGLISH LOVE OF SPORT ILLUSTRATED

Good Friday came at last in the midst of our flood-tide of success, and I determined to devote the afternoon of the general holiday to a change of programme. By the courtesy of the directors we secured the use of the Manchester race-track for a series of open-air horse races and athletic sports by the members of the company, red and white, including hurdle-races, bare-backed horsemanship, and so forth. The hold we had gained upon the popular appreciation, and the eagerness with which an Englishman starts at the mere mention of a horse-race were never more thoroughly evidenced. The day was ushered in with gloom and weeping skies, and our hearts sank within us as we realized that Jupiter Pluvius[66] was sticking to us worse than a brother and had turned on a special watering-pot for the occasion. The downpour increased as the morning wore on, and at three o'clock, the hour for commencement, the weather was simply poisonous. Both Major Burke and I were in despair, but presently we had reason to rub our eyes, and our feelings of depression gave way to astonishment. From all parts, in carriages, omnibuses, horse-cars, and on foot a huge concourse of sport-loving Britons, braving the fury of the elements, commenced to pour in upon us and in a short time our money-takers, at the six entrances to the race-ground, were wrestling for dear life with the eager throngs who fought for admission. A total attendance of nearly 30,000 was recorded, and as a reward for their fortitude the weather presently cleared up and kept fine during the progress of the sports. Again we had to register a success, and the day of our first *al fresco*[67] entertainment in Manchester is marked with a white stone in the records of the camp.

Amongst the many pleasant memories of our stay in Manchester, I shall especially cherish the hospitality extended to me by the Freemasons, who muster very strongly in the district, and at whose lodges I was frequently an honored guest. A mark of especial honor from this occult and powerful body was a public presentation of a magnificent gold watch, in the name of the Freemasons of England, by Worshipful Master—, after a performance of the Wild West. Amongst the troops of friends whom I have made in the old country, I am delighted to record that I am now and forever solid with the great and generous body of English Masons, whose Grand Master is the Prince of Wales himself.

With such little amenities our labors were enlivened and our sojourn in the smoky city made very pleasant to us. We found that each week our friendships were extending and the kindly people began to regard us more and more as their neighbors and the Wild West as an established institution amongst them. But our engagements in the land of the Stars and Stripes were fixed and unalterable as the laws of the Medes and Persians; and though the opening of bright spring weather was bringing an extraordinary pressure of business upon us, it was necessary to tear ourselves away.

HONORED BY THE MAYOR OF SALFORD

Our season in Manchester was a grand success in every way, during which I had made so many pleasant acquaintances among the citizens that notwithstanding my longing for home and America, it was with many painful feelings that we prepared to take our departure. A few days before taking leave of the scene of our magnificent triumphs I received the following letter from the Mayor of Salford:

Manchester, March 9th, 1888

Dear Sir: —It may interest you to know that I have named three streets on the New Barnes estate, on the north side of the Race-course, as follows: Cody street; Buffalo street; and Bill street, and plans for their construction will be submitted to the Salford corporation shortly.

These names will perpetuate the names of yourself and your show after your departure from Salford.

Yours truly,
Joshua Bury

The Hon. W. F. Cody,
Wild West Show, Salford.

All the Manchester papers contained, on the 19th of April, generous notices of the action of Mayor Bury in thus perpetuating my memory among the good people of his populous district. As a sample of the press comments I extract the following from the Manchester *Courier*:

Buffalo Bill's Road, Salford

Adjoining the Wild West Show at New Barnes, and between there and the cemetery, the contractor for the Ship Canal is busy converting acres of low-lying, and in some places swampy, land into good building land by placing thereon the "spoil" obtained from the big Salford dock. Within the next decade great changes in the district are manifestly impending. Long streets and broad must be formed, one of the leading and main of which is to be appropriately named Buffalo Bill's road. When completed in the near future, it will be a lengthy, broad, and busy avenue for traffic from the Ship Canal banks near Mode Wheel, into Salford. The road will commence at a point near where the buffalo, elk, etc., are at present housed, on the west side of the Wild West Show, and will extend along the boundary of the Race-course, in a due south-westerly direction, for nearly 1,000 yards. The local perpetuation of the name of Buffalo Bill and of his remarkable entertainment is thus ensured. It is expected that the Hon. W. F. Cody (Buffalo Bill) will perambulate the site of the intended road previous to his departure for New York at the beginning of next month.

A MAGNIFICENT OVATION

On Monday Evening May 1st, we gave the last indoor representation, in the presence of a vast and one of the most enthusiastic audiences I ever appeared before; bouquets were presented to various members of the company and when I appeared I met with one of the warmest receptions of my life: bouquets were thrown, handed and carried into the arena to me while the vast audience cheered, waved hats, umbrellas and handkerchiefs, jumped upon their feet, and in fact the scene was very suggestive of a pandemonium. It was fully five minutes before the noise subsided sufficiently to enable us to proceed with the performance.

Every act went with a rush and a cheer, and was received by cries of "bravo," "well done," etc. At the close of the exhibition calls were made for Red Shirt and myself, in response to which I thanked my patrons and assured them that the recollection of that evening's display of kindness would ever be fresh in my memory. Cries of "bravo Bill" and the singing of "For he's a jolly good fellow" by the entire audience brought the demonstration to a close.

On Tuesday afternoon I was given a benefit by the race-course people, on which occasion I concluded to give our outdoor performance on the race-course and despite the unfavorable weather the turn-stiles showed that nearly 50,000 people had paid admission to the grounds. This audience, like the one in the building the previous evening, was also very enthusiastic and the people seemed to vie with each other in showering applause upon the various acts and features.

A RACE FOR $2,500

Our Wild West performances in Manchester were now at a close but having two or three days to spare I concluded to accept a challenge made some days previously by Mr. B. Goodall, a noted horse breeder of Altrincham, for an international ten-mile race between his English thoroughbreds and my American bronchos, for £500 a side. The riders were J. Latham for Goodall and Tony Esquivel for me, and the conditions were that each rider should change horses without assistance at the completion of each half mile. The afternoon was fine with the exception of one fierce though fleeting rain storm. At five minutes to three o'clock thirteen of our bronchos, saddled with heavy cowboy saddles, were brought into the enclosure and about ten minutes later nine English thoroughbreds made their appearance. The men mounted their first horses at 3:20 and got away well, Latham at once taking the lead. The Englishman effected his first change with an advantage but on the next occasion he lost this and Tony went to the front. Latham, however, gained a little for some succeeding minutes. There was no question of the speed of his horses, but Tony was more adroit in changing, and before many laps were over he led the Englishman by a good two furlongs. Then for a time Tony lost ground but

Latham never succeeded in overhauling him and he passed the post 300 yards ahead, having made the remarkable time of twenty-one minutes. Wild enthusiasm was manifested throughout the race by the 20,000 spectators and at the termination of their arduous task both victorious Tony and defeated Latham were loudly cheered.

AN ENTHUSIASTIC FAREWELL

On Friday morning May 4th, at 11 a.m., amid the cheers, well wishes and hand shaking of the vast crowd who had gathered to see us depart, we pulled slowly out of the Windsor Bridge station of the Lancashire and Yorkshire Railway en route by special passenger train for Hull, where after giving our farewell English performance we were to embark for home. The time of the arrival of our train at the various stations had become generally known, and all along the entire route we were met by vast crowds who cheered and wished us God speed. Upon our arrival at Hull the crowd was so large that it was necessary to send for a squad of police to enable us to make our way through them from the station to the conveyances. On Saturday afternoon, May 5th, we gave our farewell performance in England, at Hull, before an enormous crowd and that evening at 9 o'clock our entire effects were aboard the good ship Persian Monarch which, under the command of the brave, gallant and courteous Captain Bristow, was to leave her moorings at 3 a.m. the next morning for New York. We had chartered the ship for this trip and had everything to ourselves, and all evening the vast crowds who lined the docks cheered, sang songs and wished us *bon voyage*. A great many even remained until our departure and went wild with excitement when they saw us as a company leave their shores perhaps forever.

A PATHETIC INCIDENT AT SEA

The homeward voyage was marked with one very distressing and pathetic incident to me in the loss of my favorite horse Charlie, that I had ridden for fifteen years in sunshine and in storm, in days of adversity as well as of prosperity, and to whose fleetness of foot I owed my life on more than one occasion when pursued by Indians. He stood the voyage very well, apparently, until May 14th, and even on the morning of that day when I visited him he seemed to be as well as usual.

A few minutes after leaving him, however, a groom ran to me and told me he had a chill. We did everything we could for him, but it was useless. He had lung fever, and after three days' illness he died. We could almost understand each other, and I felt very deeply. The sailors stitched him up in canvas and he lay all day Thursday, the 17th, on deck, covered with the American flag. At 8 o'clock in the evening we dropped the body, properly weighted, into the ocean. I did think of bringing him on here and burying him in his native soil, but finally concluded not to do so.

OUR ARRIVAL IN NEW YORK HARBOR

We arrived off New York harbor some time during the night of the 19th and by daylight of the 20th steamed up toward Staten Island, where we were to debark. The reception accorded us is thus graphically described by the *New York World*:

The harbor has probably never known a more picturesque scene than was witnessed yesterday morning, when the Persian Monarch steamed up from Quarantine, with Buffalo Bill standing on the captain's bridge, his tall and striking figure clearly outlined and his long hair waving in the wind, with the gaily painted and blanketed Indians leaning over the ship's rail, with the flags of all nations fluttering from the masts and connecting cables, and the band playing "Yankee Doodle" with a vim and enthusiasm which faintly indicated the joy felt by everybody connected with the Wild West exhibition, including the musicians, over the sight of home. The stolid Indians had lost their stolidity, and the white men on board declared that from the time the rising sun had enabled the redskins to discover America, or that part of it known as Staten Island, unwonted bustle and excitement had reigned supreme.

Cut Meat, American Bear, Flat Iron, Tall Horse, Kills Plenty and scores more of chiefs, braves and squaws hugged the ship's side and watched every movement of the accompanying tugs until the great vessel was towed up alongside the long wharf at Tomkinsville, and the huzzas of two thousand small boys and the noisy excitement of what seemed to be Staten Island's entire population. And it was a great day for Staten Island. So far as is known the Persian Monarch is the first great ocean steamer which has ever landed there, and this, taken in connection with the unusual nature of her passengers and her cargo, furnished abundant reason for the greatest possible commotion, excitement and disturbance whereof Mr. Wiman's small kingdom is capable.

All the teamsters for miles around had been engaged to carry the outfit of the exhibition and of the exhibitors across the island to Erastina, and the wharf was in consequence a confused commingling of express wagons, butcher carts carpenter's wagons and other kinds of vehicles, with horses attached generally on their haunches, in response to the excited demands of vociferous drivers. If this scene needed any further animation it was provided by the small boys dodging imminent death, and scores of pretty girls in their Sunday best, scurrying away from out the reach of the horses' indiscriminate hoofs.

The landing was at last effected, and Buffalo Bill, with his daughter and Major Burke, the general manager of the Wild West, Col. Ochiltree, George Trimble Davidson and several reporters, came up to the city on the tugboat Charles Stickney. Nate Salsbury, Col. Cody's partner, remained on the island and during the day the Indians and cowboys, with their tents, the Indian ponies and bucking horses, the Deadwood coach and emigrant wagons and all the paraphernalia of the show were transferred to Erastina.

I cannot describe my joy upon stepping again on the shore of beloved America. Though I had received such honors while abroad as few persons have been favored with, and scored a triumph, both socially and professionally, that may well excite my pride, yet "there is no place like home," nor is there a flag like the old flag.

With the happiness of returning to my own country again came a double portion of joy in meeting with so many old friends whose arms opened to welcome me. But of the particular pleasures of these glad meetings it does not become me to speak now, since the space at my disposal is already exhausted; suffice it therefore to say, that I am again before the American public with the Wild West Show which is now performing for the season, at Erastina, Staten Island, where we scored such a splendid success in the summer of 1886.

The following letter, which I received from General Sherman, will serve to show the influence of the Wild West Exhibitions in London, in forging closer ties of friendship, binding the mother country to her brawny and intellectual offspring, our own beloved America. In this letter the General concurs in the sentiments expressed by the several London papers as quoted in preceding pages; and I may add, that this result is more gratifying to me than all my other triumphs:

Hon. Wm. F. Cody.
Fifth Avenue Hotel
New York

Dear Cody,—. . . . . . In common with all your
countrymen, I want to let you know that I am not only
gratified, but proud of your management and general
behavior; so far as I can make out you have been modest,
graceful and dignified in all you have done to illustrate
the history of civilization on the Continent during the
past century. I am especially pleased with the graceful
and pretty compliment paid you be the Princess of
Wales, who rode with you in the Deadwood Coach
while it was attacked by the Indians, and rescued by the
Cowboys. Such things did occur in our days, but may
never again. As near as I can estimate there were in 1865
about nine and a half millions of buffaloes on the plains
between the Missouri River and the Rocky Mountains;
all are now gone-killed for their meat, their skins and
bones. This seems like desecration, cruelty and murder,
yet they have been replaced by twice as many neat cattle.
At that date there were about 165,000 Pawnees, Sioux,
Cheyennes, Kiowas and Arapahoes, who depended on
these buffaloes for their yearly food. They, too, are gone,
and have been replaced by twice or thrice as many white
men and women, who have made the earth to blossom
as the rose, and who can be counted, taxed and governed
by the laws of nature and civilization. This change has
been salutary, and will go on to the end. You have caught
one epoch of the world's history, have illustrated it in the
very heart of the modern world-London-and I want you
to feel that on this side the water we appreciate it.

This drama must end; days, years and centuries follow fast, even the drama of civilization must have an end. All I aim to accomplish on this sheet of paper is to assure you that I fully recognize your work, and that the presence of the Queen, the beautiful Princess of Wales, the Prince, and British public, are marks of favor which reflect back on America sparks of light which illuminate many a house and cabin in the land where once you guided me honestly and faithfully in 1865–6 from Fort Riley to Kearney in Kansas and Nebraska.

Sincerely, your friend,
W. T. Sherman

APPENDIX 1

Story of the Wild West

The volume of frontier biographies in which The Wild West in England *first appeared, titled* Story of the Wild West and Campfire Chats, *was published in 1888, several months after the Wild West returned from Britain. The book represented part of a concerted effort by Cody and his marketing team to capitalize on the success of the English tour. Ostensibly an account of American frontier heroism, the book uses the opening pages to frame the frontier experience in a transatlantic context. The author's preface also positions Cody as the arbiter of historical truth. His own experience, he claims, affords him a unique authority to sift fact from fiction. The result professes to be the authentic account of this "frontier pantheon" as told from the inside. The literal claims to authorship of the three biographies must be greeted with skepticism. However, the preface explains this volume's role in the Wild West's larger mission to popularize a mythic frontier experience embodied in the figure of Buffalo Bill.* The Wild West in England *is literally and figuratively the culminating chapter in* Story of the Wild West *with its project to define Buffalo Bill's Wild West exhibition as America's National Entertainment.*

The task of writing the lives of the three greatest pioneers of western settlement has been assumed by me with no little

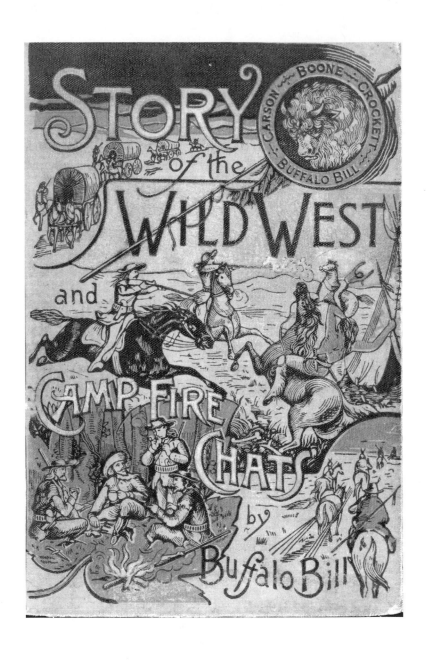

23. *Story of the Wild West* cover, 1888. Buffalo Bill Historical Center, Cody, Wyoming. 1.69.6354

Buffalo Bill's WILD WEST

AMERICA'S NATIONAL ENTERTAINMENT

CALHOUN PRINT Co.

W. F. CODY and NATE SALSBURY, Proprietors.

JOHN M. BURKE, . . . General Manager | JULE KEEN, ... Treasurer
ALBERT E. SHEIBLE, Business Representative | LEW PARKER, . . . Contracting Agent
HARRY A. LEE, ... General Agent | FRANK RICHMOND, ... Orator
NATE SALSBURY, . . . Director.

THE WILD WEST!

Hon. W. F. CODY, . . . "BUFFALO BILL."

Programme

OVERTURE.

1—GRAND PROCESSIONAL REVIEW.
2—ENTREE. Introduction of Individual Celebrities, Groups, etc.
3—RACE between Cow-boy, Mexican, and Indian on Ponies.
4—PONY EXPRESS. Illustrating the Mode of Conveying Mails on the Frontier.
5—RIFLE SHOOTING by Johnnie Baker, the Cow-boy Kid.
6—ILLUSTRATES AN ATTACK on an Emigrant Train by the Indians, and its Defense by Frontiersmen. After which A VIRGINIA REEL on Horseback by Western Girls and Cow-boys.
7—MISS ANNIE OAKLEY, Wing Shooting.
8—COW-BOY'S FUN. Throwing the Lariat. Picking Objects from the Ground while Riding at Full Speed. The Riding of Bucking Ponies and Mules by Cow-boys.
9—LILLIAN SMITH (The California Girl). Rifle Shooting.
10—LADIES' RACE by American Frontier Girls.
11—ATTACK ON THE DEADWOOD STAGE COACH by Indians. Their Repulse by Scouts and Cow-boys, Commanded by BUFFALO BILL.
12—RACE Between Sioux Indian-boys on Bareback Indian Ponies.
13—RACE Between Mexican Throughbreds.
14—HORSEBACK RIDING by American Frontier Girls.
15—PHASES OF INDIAN LIFE. Nomadic Tribe Camps on the Prairie. Attack by Hostile Tribes, followed by Scalp, War, and other Dances.
16—MUSTANG JACK, The Cow-boy Jumper.
17—BUFFALO BILL (Hon. W. F. Cody). America's Practical All-round Shot.
18—ROPING AND RIDING of Wild Texas Steers by Cow-boys and Mexicans.
19—GENUINE BUFFALO HUNT by BUFFALO BILL and Indians.
20—ATTACK ON A SETTLER'S CABIN by Hostile Indians. Repulse by Cow-boys, under the Leadership of BUFFALO BILL.
21— SALUTE.

24. *Story of the Wild West* title page, 1888. Buffalo Bill Historical Center, Cody, Wyoming. RB.F.591.C67.1888.003.

DEDICATION.

TO THE AMERICAN AND ENGLISH PUBLICS, AT WHOSE GENEROUS HANDS I
HAVE RECEIVED SO MANY FAVORS, HOSPITABLE ATTENTION
AND NUMEROUS SPECIAL KINDNESSES;

AND

TO THE ARMY OF THE FRONTIER, THE BRAVE COMRADES AND PIONEERS
WHOSE VALOROUS DEEDS, THOUGH UNWRITTEN IN THEIR COUNTRY'S
ANNALS, AND WHOSE GRAVES ARE UNMARKED SAVE BY THE
SOUGHING OAK OR THE MODEST DAISY, BUT WHO HAVE
LEFT THE HERITAGE OF A MILLION HAPPY AND
PROSPEROUS HOMES IN THE REDEEMED WEST,

THIS BOOK

IS INSCRIBED, BY ONE WHO HOLDS THEIR COURAGEOUS LIVES IN GRATEFUL
REMEMBRANCE.

W. F. CODY (BUFFALO BILL).

25. *Story of the Wild West* dedication page, 1888. Buffalo Bill Historical
Center, Cody, Wyoming. RB.F.591.C67.1888.004.

PREFACE.

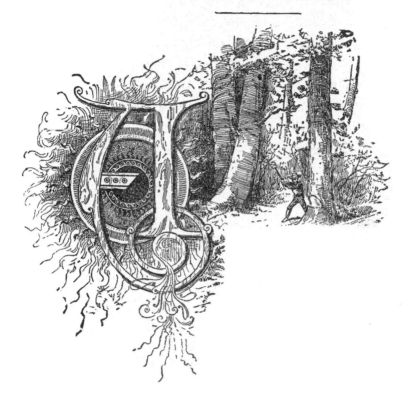

26. Opening page of preface to *Story of the Wild West*.

diffidence, surrounded as the work has been with many hard disadvantages, and obstacles of no ordinary character. Chief of these is the disadvantage of poor literary qualification, as the opportunities for acquiring an education were denied me, except such as I could obtain by unaided endeavors and a favorable association with refined persons in latter years. The obstacles of which I complain are found in the confusion of information growing out of the fact that the several biographers of Boone, Crockett and Carson have generally made quite as much use of fiction as of actual, verified incident in making up their history of these three prominent characters. The idle stories thus incorporated in their work being left so long uncontradicted have become an almost inseparable part of frontier history, since few records are accessible, or were ever made, from which a truthful account of the valorous deeds and eventful lives of these heroes may be obtained. The work thus submitted, however, has been conscientiously performed, and the care exercised, as well as the information I have collected in the course of many years, lead me to believe that the facts are here presented as nearly free from exaggeration as it is possible to give them, however great may be the study, investigation and care devoted to the work.

The life of Daniel Boone is a particularly difficult one to write. He lived at a time and in a community that permitted of little attention to the recording of events, and thus the date, and even place of his birth, is made a matter for controversy. Nor were really valorous deeds accounted as worthy of perpetuation, since the times were such as compelled every man to be a hero—a fighter ready to meet on even or uneven ground the wily savage that lurked about each frontier cabin seeking a vantage stroke to arrest the progress of settlement by merciless massacre. The modesty imbued in his nature in earlier years was little changed even by the plaudits of his admiring countrymen, when he was recognized as a leading instrument in the opening up and settlement of the Great West. The caution necessary when surrounded by savage foes made of Boone a curiously quiet man, little given to speech, and less inclined to speak of the incidents of his strangely eventful life. My chief reliance for information concerning him has, therefore, been authenticated State annals, verified by circumstances and incontestable statements of his descendants interested in preserving a truthful, though necessarily fragmentary, record of this distinguished man. It has been my good fortune, as a partial recompense for the time expended in running down idle stories concerning adventures he is said to have participated in, to meet some half a dozen pioneers of Missouri who had been intimate neighbors and friends of Boone, and to whom he related many incidents of great historical interest that I have been permitted to record for what I believe is the first time.

The life of Crockett is accessible in an elaborate work written by his own hand, though this autobiography has been furbished up and garnished with not a few unsubstantial tales that, despite their frequent exposure, still cling tenaciously to nearly all his biographies, but which I have eliminated, or repeated only to deny.

Carson's character was in more than one respect enigmatic, and many of the difficulties encountered in preparing an authentic life of Boone are found interposing between the biographer and Carson. Modesty is a becoming trait, except when it serves to obscure important incidents in the life of a justly historic personage, and in Carson this obstacle to a proper knowledge of his career is particularly conspicuous. It was my fortunate privilege to enjoy a personal acquaintance with Carson, but this intimacy gave me little advantage, for he seldom spoke of his own deeds, though I hardly think he was so different from other men as to be wholly indifferent to praise. Indeed, his desire for promotion, as explained in his biography, proves that he was susceptible of the pride that grows on exaltation.

A considerable part of Carson's life was spent in the service of the Government, and from the departmental records I have therefore extracted much of the information given herein concerning him, and which I find frequently conflicts with the statements of those who in writing his life have made facts subservient to wild exaggeration, just as many romancers have done while soberly pretending to record the incidents in my own life. Many of those who were Carson's intimates, and who were his comrades in service in the far West, were also friends of mine, and from them I gathered much reliable information concerning his adventures that I treasured up, so to speak, until this opportunity was afforded to give them currency.

While writing principally biographically, I have sought to describe that great general movement westward—that irresistible wave of emigration which, arrested for a time by the Alleghenies, rose until at last it broke over and spread away across mountain, stream and plain, leaving States in its wake, until stopped by the shores of the Pacific.

The evolution of government and of civilization, and the adaptation of one to the other, are interesting to the student of history; but particularly fascinating is the story of the reclamation of the Great West and the supplanting of the wild savages that from primeval days were lords of the country but are now become wards of the Government, whose guardianship they were forced to recognize. This story is one well calculated to inspire a feeling of pride even in the breasts of those whose sentimentality impels to commiserate the hard lot of the poor Indian; for, rising above the formerly neglected prairies of the West are innumerable monuments of thrift, industry, intelligence, and all the contributory comforts and luxuries of a peaceful and God-fearing civilization; those evidences that proclaim to a wondering world the march of the Anglo-Saxon race towards the attainment of perfect citizenship and liberal, free and stable government.

For the small part I have taken in redeeming the West from savagery, I am indebted to circumstances rather than to a natural, inborn inclination for the strifes inseparable from the life I was almost forced to choose. But to especially good fortune must I make my acknowledgments, which protected me or preserved my life a hundred times when the very hand of vengeful fate appeared to lower its grasp above my head, and hope seemed a mockery that I had turned my back upon. Good fortune has also stood ever responsive to my call since I first came before the public, and to the generous American and English peoples, as well as to kind fortune, I here pour out a full measure of profound thanks and hearty appreciation, and shall hold them gratefully in my memory as a remembrance of old friends, until the drum taps "lights out" at the close of the evening of my eventful life.

Sincerely Yours
W. F. Cody
Buffalo Bill

27. Cody's signature at the end of the preface of *Story of the Wild West*.

APPENDIX 2

Photographs, 1885–1887

The following photographs, many of them cabinet cards taken in studio settings in London, portray the development of William Cody's celebrity status, beginning in the mid-1880s, as well as some of the most notable figures from the Wild West's English tour. With its huge cast and many featured players, the Wild West transformed show people such as Annie Oakley, Red Shirt, and Buck Taylor into popular culture icons. Collectively these images and the thousands more like them suggest why Buffalo Bill's Wild West so effectively capitalized on an emerging visual culture.

28. William F. Cody shaking hands with Sitting Bull, ca. 1885. Buffalo Bill Historical Center, Cody, Wyoming. P.6.247.

29. Cody with Pawnee scouts to his left and Sioux chiefs to his right. *From left to right*: Brave Chief, Eagle Chief, Knife Chief, Young Chief, Cody, American Horse, Rocky Bear, Flies Above, and Long Wolf, 1886. Buffalo Bill Historical Center, Cody, Wyoming. P.6.878.

COLONEL W. F. CODY,
" Buffalo Bill "
ELLIOTT & FRY, Copyright 55&56, BAKER ST LONDON W

30. William F. Cody, from Elliot and Fry, London, 1887.
Buffalo Bill Historical Center, Cody, Wyoming. P.6.26.

31. William F. Cody, studio portrait from Elliot and Fry, London, 1887. Buffalo Bill Historical Center, Cody, Wyoming. P.6.826.

32. View of the cast of Buffalo Bill's Wild West, including
William F. Cody, Nate Salsbury, Johnny Baker, Annie Oakley,
Buck Taylor, John Burke, and John Nelson, June 1887.
Buffalo Bill Historical Center, Cody, Wyoming. P.6.205.

33. Wild West Show's managers and pressmen, including
Nate Salsbury (*pointing with cane*) and John Burke (*seated, center*),
ca. 1887. Buffalo Bill Historical Center, Cody, Wyoming. P.69.810.

34. William F. Cody sitting outside tent in civilian dress, ca. 1887.
Buffalo Bill Historical Center, Cody, Wyoming. P.69.745.

35. William F. Cody on Charlie, ca. 1887. Buffalo Bill Historical Center, Cody, Wyoming. P.6.25

Copyright. Woodburytype.

RED SHIRT,
The Fighting Chief of the Sioux Nation.

BUFFALO BILL'S WILD WEST.

36. Red Shirt, ca. 1887.
Buffalo Bill Historical Center, Cody, Wyoming. P.6.27.

Copyright.   Woodburytype.

RED SHIRT,
The Fighting Chief of the Sioux Nation.

BUFFALO BILL'S WILD WEST.

37. Red Shirt, ca. 1887.
Buffalo Bill Historical Center, Cody, Wyoming. P.6.28.

38. Buffalo Bill's Wild West cowboys, including Johnny Baker, John Boyer, Cyrus Hagadone, Billy Johnson, Dick Johnson, Long Haired Hank, and Jim Kid Willoughby, ca. 1887. Buffalo Bill Historical Center, Cody, Wyoming. P.6.86.

39. Serapio Rivera, ca. 1887. Buffalo Bill Historical Center, Cody, Wyoming. P.6.32.

Copyright.   Woodburytype.

BUCK TAYLOR,

"King of the Cow-boys."

BUFFALO BILL'S WILD WEST.

40. Buck Taylor, ca. 1887. Buffalo Bill Historical Center,
Cody, Wyoming. P.6.34.

Copyright.   Woodburytype.

LITTLE CHIEF,
Chief of the Ogalallas.

BUFFALO BILL'S WILD WEST.

41. Little Chief, ca. 1887.
Buffalo Bill Historical Center, Cody, Wyoming. P.6.36.

J. WOOD, Photo., 208 Bowery, N. Y.

42. Annie Oakley, ca. 1887. Buffalo Bill Historical Center,
Cody, Wyoming. P.69.1590.

Copyright.   Woodburytype.

MISS ANNIE OAKLEY,
"Little Sure-Shot."

BUFFALO BILL'S WILD WEST.

43. Annie Oakley wearing her shooting awards, ca. 1887.
Buffalo Bill Historical Center, Cody, Wyoming. P.6.30.

Copyright.   Woodburytype.

JOHN NELSON AND FAMILY,
Scout, Interpreter and Guide.

BUFFALO BILL'S WILD WEST.

44. John Y. Nelson and family, ca. 1887.
Buffalo Bill Historical Center, Cody, Wyoming. P.6.46.

162   APPENDIX 2

45. Four Indian women and three children, including John Nelson's
wife and Red Rose, ca. 1888. Buffalo Bill Historical Center,
Cody, Wyoming. P.6.60.

Copyright.   Woodburytype.

WA-KA-CHA-SHA (RED ROSE),
The Girl-pet of the Sioux.

BUFFALO BILL'S WILD WEST.

46. Wa-Ka-Cha-Sha (Red Rose, the Girl-pet of the Sioux), ca. 1887. Buffalo Bill Historical Center, Cody, Wyoming. P.6.43.

GOOD EAGLE,
Chief of the Cheyennes.

BUFFALO BILL'S WILD WEST.

47. Good Eagle wearing peace medals, ca. 1887.
Buffalo Bill Historical Center, Cody, Wyoming. P.6.41.

Copyright. Woodburytype.

FLIES ABOVE,
Chief of the Cut-off Band of Sioux.

BUFFALO BILL'S WILD WEST.

48. Flies Above, ca. 1887.
Buffalo Bill Historical Center, Cody, Wyoming. P.6.42.

Copyright.   Woodburytype.

BLUE HORSE,
Chief of the Shoshones.

BUFFALO BILL'S WILD WEST.

49. Blue Horse, ca. 1887.
Buffalo Bill Historical Center, Cody, Wyoming. P.6.39.

50. Bennie Irving, "The Smallest Cow Boy in the World," ca. 1887. Denver Public Library, NS-108.

APPENDIX 3

Promotion, Reception, and the Popular Press

The materials included here depict various aspects of Wild West publicity, including both the show's marketing efforts and how it was perceived in the popular press and by members of the public. The Wild West program, the American Exhibition commemorative book, and promotional posters all highlight how the show both depended upon and promoted celebrity culture. U.S. military leaders, Queen Victoria and her family, and the Wild West's featured performers all were grist for the show's marketing machine.

Always at the center of the Wild West branding strategy, Cody made himself available for personal appearances among London's cultural and political elites. Two personal invitations—one real, the other a practical joke—speak to Cody's status on the London social scene. Press coverage of Cody and the Wild West tended to reinforce the international theme of The Wild West in England. *Cartoons in* Punch *and* Puck, *as well as other satiric publications, found the dynamics of the cultural encounter an irresistible subject. But even straightforward newspaper accounts saw the Wild West as part of a larger framework of international relations. While Cody's narrative quotes freely from British newspapers, some samples of American press coverage are included here as well. They show how the Wild West abroad evoked nationalist sentiment at home. These materials give evidence of a highly sophisticated effort at mass marketing and public relations, all of which culminated in the publication of* The Wild West in England.

Satiric sketch from *Life Magazine*, May 1887

BUFFALO BILL AT WINDSOR

The Queen having expressed her wish to the Chum to Potentates that the Wild West Show should appear before Her Majesty at Windsor Castle, your correspondent escorted that body into the royal presence on Tuesday last.

A large audience of Nobles had assembled to do honor to the aristocratic redmen of the far West, and the Royal Maroon Band played "Lo, the Conquering Hero Comes," as the tribes bowed their respects to Her Majesty. The braves in honor of the occasion wore a new coat of paint and the regulation three feathers in their back hair—a costume which was at once effective and gentlemanly, if, as an old authority on dress has said, "A gentleman's dress is never conspicuous."

A large space in front of the castle had been cleared for the performance, and after a light luncheon Mr. Nate Salsbury mounted a pedestal from which the statue of William the Conqueror had been temporarily removed, and explained to Her Majesty that the Comanche tribe from the suburbs of Boston, would now see how near they could come to running over Prince Battenberg without really hurting him.

This was followed by an exhibition at shooting, when Buffalo Bill shot the Koh-i-noor out of the Queen's Spring crown seven times running, much to the delight of her Majesty and the wonder of the assembled Nobles.

Several cow-ladies were then introduced; giving British aristocracy a fair imitation of high life in New York city. The

51. Opening page from American Exhibition commemorative volume, 1887. Buffalo Bill Historical Center, Cody, Wyoming. PICT0003.

Queen was much surprised at the refined way in which American ladies do their shopping on bucking ponies, and when one of the young ladies with auburn hair showed with what facility American girls use their firearms when their young gentleman friends decline to take them to the opera, the royal family was nearly carried away with delight.

At the request of the Chum, Mr. Buffalo Bill gave a graphic representation of New York's first families on their way to church. The old camp-wagon was brought out and Mr. Cody disguised as Mr. Vanastorbilt, stepped up on the box and started the horses off. Grace Church was represented by a canvas tent, and Fourteenth Street was shown by a pole stuck in the ground. The Queen could hardly restrain herself when the team ran away, and the nimble Buffalo Bill, tying a lasso around his

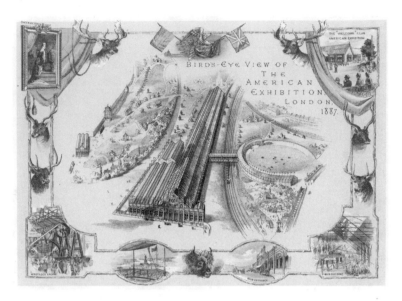

52. Page from American Exhibition commemorative volume,
"Bird's-Eye View of the American Exhibition, London, 1887."
Buffalo Bill Historical Center, Cody, Wyoming. PICT0001.

waist, stopped them by casting the noose over a stump on which
were growing some wistaria vines and which was supposed to
represent a lamp-post. Her Majesty had heard of Mr. Vanastorbilt, but never supposed he was so clever a man.

Then, as the carriage neared Fourteenth Street, the low,
ominous war-cry of the Sioux Indians was heard, and the faithful picture of New York life that then followed, with its awful
butchery and bellowing of buffaloes on Union Square, needs
no description for your readers who have grown so familiar
with it in the daily round of life. Suffice it to say that the British aristocracy fairly yelled with joy as Mr. Vanastorbilt slew
file after file of the attacking party, losing only his scalp and
four children in the melee.

The exhibition was closed by a pastoral scene showing how

53. Page from American Exhibition commemorative volume,
"Her Majesty Queen Victoria at the 'Wild West' Exhibition," 1887.
Buffalo Bill Historical Center, Cody, Wyoming. PICT0008.

the Indians and whites live peacefully together in Philadelphia, with an allegorical tableau at the end, showing a six-foot Comanche labeled William Penn, standing beside a small four-inch stage sword, the significance of which Her Majesty immediately perceived, for as she left the grounds she spoke of the pathetic rendering of the old proverb, "The Comanche is mightier than the dagger."

In return for the pleasure he had given her, Buffalo Bill and "Potato-Faced-Charley" were invested with the Order of the Bath—which the Indian declined from natural scruples, not understanding the idiomatic significance of the decoration.

On the whole the day passed off pleasantly, and there were no disturbances other than a slight misunderstanding between the Prince of Wales and a young Sioux brave, in which the Prince's baldness served him in good stead.

54. Page from American Exhibition commemorative volume,
"Stars of the Show," 1887. Buffalo Bill Historical Center,
Cody, Wyoming. PICT0011.

It is rumored that the National Gallery of London has offered one of the Indians a large salary if he will annex himself to the Turner Gallery, and exhibit the sunset that he wears on the small of his back when he goes to war. The trustees of the Gallery claim to have internal evidence that the painting is by the hand of the master, and that it must be had at any cost.

It seems to me that this affords the United States a chance to settle the fishery question by swapping off the artistic brave for justice—and the only way to get justice from the English Government is to pay for it.

Her Majesty's desire to see these untutored savages in their native lair may induce her to visit New York next season, in which case she will probably be under the management of D'Ovlv Carte.

Carlyle Smith.

55. Program for Buffalo Bill's Wild West, 1887. Buffalo Bill Historical Center, Cody, Wyoming. 1887Prgrm.03.

56. Promotional poster with endorsements from leading U.S. military officers, 1887. Buffalo Bill Historical Center, Cody, Wyoming. 1.69.127.

57. Promotional poster of distinguished visitors to the show, 1887.
Buffalo Bill Historical Center, Cody, Wyoming. 1.69.130.

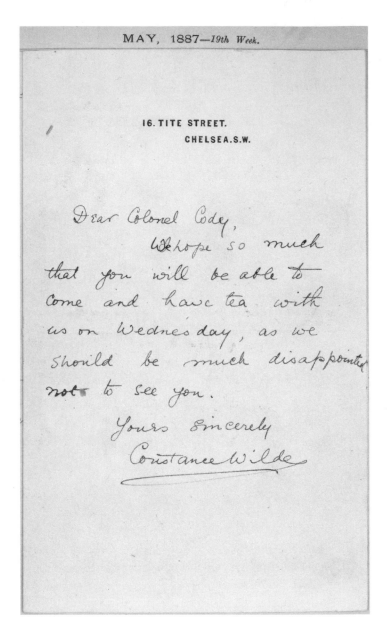

MAY, 1887—*19th Week.*

16. TITE STREET.
CHELSEA. S.W.

Dear Colonel Cody,
We hope so much that you will be able to come and have tea with us on Wednesday, as we should be much disappointed not to see you.
Yours sincerely
Constance Wilde

58. Invitation from Oscar Wilde's wife, Constance, May 1887.
Buffalo Bill Historical Center, Cody, Wyoming.
Invitations and Letters, 1887–1888-08.

WINDSOR CASTLE
July. 1st 1887

Dear Bill —
Come up at four and bring Red Shirt with you. The beer is on ice. Don't fail
Ever yours
Vic.
R.

Burn this

59. Hoax invitation purportedly from Queen Victoria, July 1887.
Buffalo Bill Historical Center, Cody, Wyoming.
Invitations & Letters-1887–1888-13.

60. Postcard from Cody friend Matt O'Brien, June 23, 1887.
Buffalo Bill Historical Center, Cody, Wyoming. MS6.1.B.2.20.01.a1.

61. Ad in *The Penney Illustrated Paper and Illustrated Times*, May 7, 1887.

From *Life Magazine*, May 1888

The career of Buffalo William in England ought to teach our Anglomaniacs a useful lesson. The Wild West Show has done more to stimulate Americanism among the republicans who travel abroad, and to inculcate respect for Americans, as Americans, among foreigners, than has ever been accomplished by our ministers at the European courts. Indeed, it is so universal a custom for our representatives and tourists abroad, and

62. Images in *The Graphic*, May 21, 1887.

particularly in England, to bow down before foreign customs, ape foreign manners and admire foreign institutions, that it is little wonder that we should be regarded as an inferior people, being so willing, as we most of us are, to admit it. By the basilar principles of Americanism, as laid down in the Declaration of Independence, upon which our Constitution is founded, we are a race of sovereigns who profess to hold up our heads before kings and princes as proudly as they. And yet scarcely an American travels abroad but esteems it the highest honor he has yet achieved to be permitted to bow reverently before a fat and gross little man, the third-rate intellect and fourth-rate morals, because that same fat and gross little man is heir apparent to the British throne; and at the same time a barnacle upon the nation, a pauper upon the people, a mere figure-head

63. "The Other Side of the Question—Yankee-Mania in England," from *Judge Magazine*, 1887. Buffalo Bill Historical Center, Cody, Wyoming. MS6.3367.

for an outworn system of government that has already ceased to exist, same in name.

BUFFALO BILL WENT TO ENGLAND
AS A PLAIN SHOWMAN

He made no pretences, but his reputation as an American, in what the name implies as distinguishing him from a sycophant, or a republican who would like to be a subject, had gone before him. He did not wait upon the Prince of Wales, but that fat and gross little man waited upon him; and, though Buffalo Bill was lionized and made much of by that element of English society that most Americans—alas! that we should be obliged to say it—are proud to grovel before, he abated not one whit from his simple dignity as a man and a republican. If every American followed the example of William F. Cody, the

BUFFALO BILL'S WILD WEST SHOW AT THE AMERICAN EXHIBITION, EARL'S COURT

64. "Buffalo Bill's Wild West Show at the American Exhibition, Earl's Court," from *The Graphic*, May 7, 1887. Buffalo Bill Historical Center, Cody, Wyoming. MS6.3353.

184   APPENDIX 3

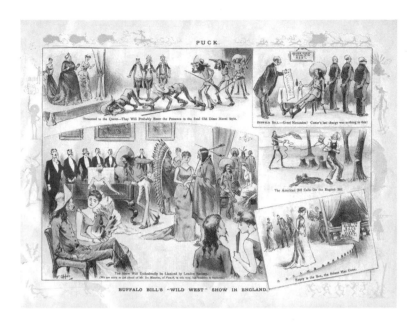

65. "Buffalo Bill's Wild West Show in England," from *Puck Magazine*, April 13, 1887. Buffalo Bill Historical Center, Cody, Wyoming. MS6.3351.

Buffalo Bill of the Western prairies, American influence would mount high in foreign places, and the world would soon realize that the real republican is a nobler order of man than can be bred from a subject people.

And, as we are upon the subject of Buffalo Bill, it is worthwhile to draw attention to the scout's funeral oration over his old horse "Charlie," that died at sea on the journey to America. Cooper never put a prettier sentiment into the mouths of any of his picturesque frontiersmen or romantic savages. Said the scout, winding up the oration, just before the body of this faithful steed, that had carried him on many famous rides through the perilous Indian country of the far West, was committed to the deep: "Charlie, but for your willing speed and tireless courage I would many years ago have lain as low as you are now,

66. "The Queen's Visit to the East End," from *The Graphic*, May 21, 1887. Buffalo Bill Historical Center, Cody, Wyoming. MS6.2277.

and my Indian foe have claimed you for his slave. Yet you have never failed me, Charlie, old fellow! I have had many friends, but very few of whom I could say that. Men tell me you had no soul, but if there be a Heaven, and scouts can enter there, I'll wait at the gate for you, old friend!"

From the *Washington Post*, October 1888

GEORGE WILLIAM CURTIS ON BUFFALO BILL

No one who sees the "Wild West Show" can wonder that Buffalo Bill deeply impressed our English cousins. The old Viking and Berserker survives in John Bull. A certain savage strain lingers in his tastes, which Taine sensitively apprehended. His prize-fights and Mohawk rioting, his tiger and elephant hunting, his excursions to shoot buffalo and grizzly bears, are in one view manly sports, and in another brutal survivals. Then Mayfair in London is sated. It has exhausted every resource of costly luxury. It is jaded, and the sudden appearance of living

67. "The Queen's Visit to the Wild West Show at West Brompton," from *The Graphic*, May 21, 1887. Buffalo Bill Historical Center, Cody, Wyoming.

Indians, and the life of the far West as it is actually seen, was an agreeable shock of surprise, and gave it a real emotion.

The only serious objection to the exhibition that the Easy Chair has heard is that which was urged almost with tearful earnestness by one of the most reasonable and excellent of women. It is pitiful and wicked, she said, that just as a hopeful effort is made to interest the intelligent country in the civilization of the Indian, his squalid savagery should be made a circus spectacle to degrade him in the minds of the people, and to stimulate all the worst dime novel tastes and tendencies among boys. But the good critic did not speak from observation or knowledge. Had she seen the spectacle she would have discovered that the Indian was not degraded in her mind

68. "A Sickening Blow to the Anglomaniac," from *Life Magazine*,
June 23, 1887. From the collection of Doug Wheeler,
http://superitch.com/?p=6183.

by showing himself as he is. Indeed, the performance is merely like one of his own games upon the plains, and he does not lose in dignity. On the contrary, the spectacle leaves probably a more accurate impression of the Indian than can be gained except by a visit to the plains.

Certainly, that [reflect] supposed by the critic is not produced, and it is not at all of the kind injurious to the colored people which is due to the Ethiopian minstrels. It is, indeed, the raw material of the Indian that is seen, and not that which has been already influenced in a degree by civilization. But no one seems to hold sounder or humaner views of the Indian, or of the duties that we owe him, and the manner in which they should be discharged, than Buffalo Bill.

69. "On Their Return," from *Puck Magazine*, May 25, 1887.
National Cowboy and Western Heritage Museum, 1996.027.1461.141.

70. "Days with Celebrities," from *Moonshine*, May 21, 1887.
From the collection of Doug Wheeler,
http://superitch.com/?p=6183.

NOTES

Editor's Introduction

1. American painter George Catlin (1792–1872) had successfully toured European cities in 1839 displaying his portraits of Native Americans. He later added living Indians to his exhibition. P. T. Barnum toured Europe in the mid-1840s with Tom Thumb. Like Cody, his visit to England included an audience with Queen Victoria.

2. Similarly, Cody fails to include any mention of Annie Oakley in his account of the London season. This decision may be related to the fact that Oakley and her husband left the show in October and had not returned by the time *Story of the Wild West* was published.

3. President Grover Cleveland was among those Sitting Bull met during his stay in Washington DC.

4. See Nicholas Black Elk's and John G. Neihardt's *Black Elk Speaks: Being the Life Story of a Holy Man of the Oglala Sioux* and Luther Standing Bear's *My People the Sioux*.

5. *The Wild West in England*, [131].

6. *Buffalo Bill's America*, 199.

7. Admission to the American Exhibition cost one shilling. Two shilling sixpence covered admission to the exhibition and the Wild West. Separate admission to the Wild West cost two shillings for a seat and one shilling for standing room.

8. Turner, *Frontier and Section*, 38.

9. *The Wild West in England*, [39].

10. *The Wild West in England*, [38].

11. *The Wild West in England*, [46].

12. *The Wild West in England*, [25].

13. *The Wild West in England*, [25].

14. *The Wild West in England*, [26].

15. In addition to the cast of hundreds and the menagerie of elk, deer, buffalo, cattle, and horses, the show employed an army of workers to build the twenty-thousand-seat arena and encampment to house performers and stock. Hundreds of tons of soil were shipped in to re-create a western landscape in the arena.

16. *The Wild West in England*, [36].

17. *The Wild West in England*, [65].

18. *The Wild West in England*, [65].

19. Found in Twain's 1895 essay "The Literary Offenses of Fenimore Cooper."

20. *The Wild West in England*, [76].

21. *The Wild West in England*, [77].

22. *The Wild West in England*, [74].

23. *Quoted in Buffalo Bill's British Wild West.*

24. *Quoted in Buffalo Bill's British Wild West.*

25. *The Wild West in England*, [181].

The Wild West in England

1. This was the final season of the Buffalo Bill Combination, which toured the country performing "border dramas" for a decade. Essentially western melodramas starring Buffalo Bill as himself, these plays can be seen as precursors to the Wild West shows.

2. Literally "cowmen," these Mexican horsemen were the original North American cowboys, first encountered by Anglophone settlers in Texas in the 1820s.

3. The actual opening date was May 19.

4. Cody's first Wild West show, the "Rocky Mountain and Prairie Exhibition," was a partnership with W. F. "Doc" Carver that dissolved after one season. The relationship ended acrimoniously, which may account for Cody's failure to mention Carver in this account.

5. Nate Salsbury (1846–1902) was a theatrical manager who formed his own company, Salsbury's Troubadours, in 1874. He produced comic burlesques with considerable success in the United

States, Britain, and Australia for a decade before joining the Wild West as managing partner in 1884.

6. Located in east central Georgia, Andersonville Prison was also known as Fort Sumter. It opened as a prison early in 1864 and gained infamy for the large number of Union prisoners who died there of malnutrition and disease (more than a fourth of the total).

7. A system of prisoner exchange was conducted during the middle stages of the Civil War. Ulysses S. Grant put a stop to the practice in 1864, arguing that it only served to prolong the war.

8. Founded by Moses Kimball in 1841, the Boston Museum served as a theater while exhibiting fine art and wax figures. It also contained a natural history museum and live animal exhibits. It closed in 1903.

9. A company of actors associated with a particular theater, which use a set repertoire of plays.

10. With the Salsbury partnership the enterprise took on the name "Buffalo Bill's Wild West" for the first time.

11. Chief Sitting Bull (ca. 1831–1890) was a Lakota chief and the most well-known Native American to participate in Buffalo Bill's Wild West. Sitting Bull gained renown during the Great Sioux War of 1876–77 when he led his Hunkpapa band in multiple battles, including Little Bighorn. After the war Sitting Bull led his followers to Canada rather than surrender. They returned to the United States and surrendered in 1881. His involvement with the Wild West was limited to four months in 1884. Unlike the rest of the Show Indians, Sitting Bull performed by riding around the arena only once during each program. He was also able to trade on his celebrity status by charging for his autograph and to have his picture taken.

12. Cody indicates that participation in Custer's Last Stand (or the Battle of the Little Bighorn) was an important litmus test for the Show Indians. It played a similar role in his own career even though he had no direct involvement in the battle. In July 1876, Cody was involved in a skirmish at War Bonnet Creek in which he killed a Cheyenne named Yellow Hair. Cody used the incident to associate his own public persona with that of the newly martyred George Armstrong Custer. He commissioned and starred in a play titled *The Red Right Hand, or First Scalp for Custer*, which toured the country later that same year.

13. William Levi "Buck" Taylor (1857–1924), billed as the "King of the Cowboys," was a featured performer in the Wild West beginning with its first season. At 'six-foot-five-inches in height, Taylor made a striking figure. His performance centered on horsemanship skills such as picking objects off the ground on horseback at full gallop. Born in Texas and orphaned at an early age, he made his way to Nebraska working as a cowpuncher, eventually finding employment on Cody's ranch. He was also featured in a number of western dime novels beginning with *Buck Taylor, King of the Cowboys* written by Prentiss Ingraham and published in 1887. John Y. Nelson came to the Wild West with a background as a trapper and guide. In addition to performing in the show, he served as an interpreter. Married to an Oglala Sioux woman, Nelson's wife and five children also performed with the Wild West.

14. The World's Industrial and Cotton Centennial Exposition was Cody and Salsbury's first association with a world's fair. They went on to have great success at similar events, including the American Exhibition of 1887, the Paris Exposition Universelle of 1889, and the Chicago World's Columbian Exhibition of 1893.

15. Erastus Wiman (1834–1904) was a businessman and promoter who owned a summer resort on Staten Island called Erastina. This represented the Wild West's first successful attempt at an extended stay in a single location.

16. Built in 1879, this first incarnation of Madison Square Garden had a seating capacity of ten thousand. Cody and Salsbury used this opportunity (an indoor arena and a New York audience already familiar with the Wild West exhibition) to reinvent the show. They hired artistic director Steele Mackaye, who incorporated the existing acts into The Drama of Civilization: A Panoramic History of American Colonization that culminated in the settling of the mountain west.

17. The allusion to Shakespeare's *Hamlet* references one of Hamlet's soliloquy's, which reads: "So excellent a king; that was, to this, / Hyperion to a satyr; so loving to my mother / That he might not beteem the winds of heaven / Visit her face too roughly. Heaven and earth! / Must I remember? Why, she would hang on him, / As if increase of appetite had grown / By what it fed on."

18. Among these: Mark Twain and the organizers of the American Exhibition.

19. First conceived in 1885 by English entrepreneur John Whitley, the American Exhibition of Arts, Inventions, Manufactures, and Resources of the United States was modeled on London's 1851 Crystal Palace Exhibition. It was distinct from other world's fairs, however, in its exclusive focus on one country. Troubled by logistical and financial challenges from the start, the exhibition was widely perceived as having been saved by the partnership with The Wild West.

20. Red Shirt was an Oglala Sioux from the Red Cloud Agency. He played a pivotal role in the success of the Wild West as the most visible and, ultimately, most well-known Indian in the show, after Sitting Bull.

21. An indispensable element of the Wild West from its first year, the band, led by cornet player William Sweeney, played a key role in the show with its music serving as a musical accompaniment to the action in the arena. The sixteen-piece band included a combination of clarinets, cornets, trombones, horns, a piccolo, a tuba, and drums.

22. Arta Lucille Cody (1866–1904).

23. A town on the southern bank of the Thames River.

24. John M. Burke (1842–1917) was also known as "Arizona John" and "Major" John Burke, although he did not have a military record. Burke is first mentioned in Cody's 1879 autobiography as the man who took over the publicity for the Cody theatrical company after the departure of Ned Buntline. He later served as general manager of the Buffalo Bill Combination and then Buffalo Bill's Wild West. Burke had been working for Cody for nearly fifteen years at the time of the English tour; he eventually worked with Cody for thirty-four years. He is credited with contributing significantly to the success of the show through innovative marketing and savvy management of the press.

25. Lord Ronald Gower (Lord Ronald Charles Sutherland-Leveson-Gower, 1845–1916). A British aristocrat and Liberal politician for Sutherland from 1867 to 1874, he was also a noted sculptor and writer.

26. The first rail line of the London Underground, completed in 1863, was the world's first underground railway. This was a novelty for

Cody as the United States did not have its first underground system until 1897.

27. A relatively new form of oil-burning light. Lucigen lights could illuminate up to a 150-yard radius.

28. The horse-drawn taxi of urban Victorian England, the Hansom cab, was patented by Joseph Hansom in 1834.

29. A street near the Thames River in the City of Westminster, London, the Strand was a hub of Victorian cultural life. A number of popular theaters and the residences of many notable writers were located on this street.

30. Located on the north bank of the Thames estuary opposite the town of Gravesend, this fort served a strategic role in national defense from the sixteenth through the early twentieth centuries.

31. Variant of "halyard."

32. Sir Henry Irving (John Henry Brodribb, 1838–1905) was a leading proponent of English classical theater and the first actor to receive a knighthood. He was actor-manager at the Lyceum Theatre, where he worked closely with theater manager Bram Stoker for many years. In addition to his public endorsement of the Wild West before its arrival in England, Irving fostered Cody's relations with the theatrical community throughout his stay in London.

33. A Muslim warrior caste active during medieval times, especially during the Crusades.

34. Richard Turpin (ca. 1705–1739) was a notorious English highwayman. His life received various literary treatments, including William Ainsworth's 1834 novel, *Rookwood*, alluded to here.

35. Theodore Winthrop (1828–1861) was an American writer whose novel *John Brent* was based on his own travels in the far West.

36. King Henri IV (1553–1610) ruled France from 1589 to 1610.

37. Georgia Duffy joined the Wild West in 1886 and, along with Della Ferrell, was billed in the program as part of the "Beautiful Rancheras." She was married to another cast member, cowboy Tom Duffy.

38. June 20, 1887, marked the fiftieth anniversary of Queen Victoria's accession to the throne.

39. This list of distinguished persons is characteristic of the Wild West's marketing strategy, which utilized images of famous visitors in show posters and other promotional materials. The recently knighted Sir Francis Philip Cunliffe Owen (1828–1894) had organized several successful exhibitions in the 1880s and became first director of the Imperial Institute, founded in 1887. Lord Alfred Henry Paget (1816–1888) was a former member of Parliament (representing Lichfield) and an official in the royal household. Lord Charles William de la Poer Beresford (1846 1919) was a member of Parliament for East Marylebone, London, and an admiral in the Royal Navy. Grand Duke Michael Mikhailovich of Russia (1861–1929) was a first cousin of Alexander III of Russia. He was among the group of foreign dignitaries visiting London to attend the Queen's jubilee celebrations.

Sir Francis Knollys (1837–1924) served as private secretary to the Prince of Wales. Lady Alice Bective (?–1928) was the wife of Thomas Taylour, Earl of Bective. Lady Randolph Churchill (Jeanette Jerome, 1854–1921), the American wife of Lord Randolph Henry Spencer Churchill, was a leading London socialite, playwright, and author. She was the mother of Winston Churchill. Mrs. J. W. Mackay (Marie Louise Hungerford) was the wife of John William Mackay, an American financier.

40. "See, refer to, consult" is a direction to the reader to refer to some other heading, passage, or work (or to a table, diagram, etc.) for fuller or further information (from the OED).

41. A notorious divorce case that caused a sensation in the English popular press in 1885.

42. William Ewart Gladstone (1809–1898), the four-time prime minister of Great Britain, was between his third and fourth stints as prime minister at the time of his visit in 1887. His visit was widely reported in the London press and proved to be a marketing boon to the Wild West.

43. Albert Edward, Prince of Wales (1841–1910), the eldest son of Queen Victoria and Prince Albert, later became king of Great Britain from 1901 to 1910. During Victoria's extended seclusion after the death of her husband, it fell to Edward to be the face of the Crown. He was a patron of the arts as well as an enthusiastic sportsman, so his

endorsement of the Wild West gave the exhibition credibility among English high society. George William Frederick Charles (1819–1904) was the second Duke of Cambridge. Wilson Barrett (1846–1904) was a prominent English stage actor and playwright. Christopher Sykes (1831–1898) was an English aristocrat who had a long but undistinguished career as a member of Parliament for Beverley and East Riding. Herbert Gladstone (1854–1930) was the son of William Gladstone and a member of Parliament from 1880 to 1910. Mrs. Chas. Matthews (Elizabeth or "Lizzie") Davenport, (?–1899) was the American-born wife of actor and playwright Charles James Mathews (1803–1878). Edmund Hodgson Yates (1831–1894) was a prominent writer and journal editor. A founder of the American Bar Association, Edward John Phelps (1822–1900) was envoy to the Court of Saint James from 1885 to 1889. American Thomas MacDonald Waller (1840–1924) served as consul-general in London from 1885 to 1889. Sir Charles Wyndham (Charles Culverwell, 1937–1919) was an English actor and theater manager who interrupted his stage career to serve as a surgeon for the Confederate Army during the U.S. Civil War. Sir Edward Levy-Lawson (1833–1903) was the owner of the *London Daily Telegraph*. Oscar and Constance Wilde, widely regarded as the center of the London cultural scene, were among the cultural elites who hosted Cody in their home during his London stay. The couple had two children (one in 1885 and the other in 1886). In the popular press Cody's celebrity was sometimes compared to Wilde's. Amalia Mignon Hauck (Minnie Hauk, 1851–1929) was an American operatic soprano. Mary Anderson (1859–1940) was an American actress who had several successful stints on the London stage in the 1880s. Emma Nevada Palmer (Emma Wixom, 1850–1940) was an American opera singer. Cora Urquhart Brown-Potter (1859–1936) was an American stage actress. She had arrived in London in 1886 to pursue her acting career. Henry Labouchere (1831–1912) was a British member of Parliament and journalist.

44. Frank Richmond served as orator, introducing each act and providing a running narrative context throughout the performance. He died in Spain in 1890 on the Wild West's second tour abroad in the midst of an influenza and typhoid outbreak.

45. James Fenimore Cooper (1789–1851) was among the first U.S. novelists to establish a viable transatlantic literary career. Noted for his novels about the American frontier, he is best known for his Leatherstocking Tales featuring Natty Bumppo, a literary archetype of frontier manhood. Because of his penchant for historical romances, Cooper was often compared to Sir Walter Scott, the Scottish novelist.

46. A view or scene as it strikes the eye at a glance (from the OED).

47. Gilbert H. Bates was a veteran of the Civil War serving as a sergeant in the Union Army. He first achieved notoriety when he undertook a fourteen-hundred-mile trek to bear the Stars and Stripes throughout the American South in 1868. In 1883 Cody hired Bates to be the flag bearer for the Wild West.

48. *coram publico*: German, for "publicly."

49. Antonio Jose Esquival was known as the "champion vaquero." In addition to his cowboy role, Jim Kidd was the husband of Wild West star sharpshooter Lillian Smith. Mitchell and Webb refer to cast members Jim Mitchell and Tom Webb.

50. This was, in fact, a used stagecoach, which Cody purchased and had restored. Beginning in 1876 with the gold rush taking hold in the Black Hills of Dakota Territory, the Deadwood stagecoach carried passengers along the Cheyenne-Deadwood Stage road. The stage became legendary for the number of times it was attacked and robbed by Indians and bandits, making it a perfect set piece for Cody's dramatic reenactments.

51. Mahomet is an archaic spelling of Muhammad. The proverb "If the mountain will not come to Mahomet, Mahomet must go to the mountain" refers to the tale of Muhammad, who commanded a mountain to move as proof of divine authority but found providential design in God's refusal.

52. Princess Beatrice (1857–1944) was the youngest child of Queen Victoria and Prince Albert, married to Prince Henry Maurice of Battenberg (1858–1896). Anne Home-Drummond was the Dowager Duchess of Athole (1814–1897). Ethel Cadogan (1852–1930) was a British courtier, serving as a maid-of-honour to Queen Victoria during this time. Sir Henry Ponsonby was the queen's private secretary.

53. John Bright (1811–1889) was an influential British reform politician who advocated for the working class over the course of his long career.

54. *Punch,* a British weekly magazine with a satiric focus founded in 1842, took its name from the sock puppet Mr. Punch.

55. James Gillespie Blaine (1830–1893) was a Republican politician and diplomat. He served as speaker of the house and ran unsuccessfully for president in 1884. Two years after his visit to the Wild West he was appointed secretary of state. Joseph Pulitzer (1847–1911), the publisher of the *St. Louis Post-Dispatch* and the *New York World,* had stepped down from his congressional seat the year before. Chauncey Mitchell Depew (1834–1928) was the president of the New York Central Hudson River Railroad Company. He later became a U.S. senator. Murat Halstead (1829–1908) was an American newspaper editor and writer. Joseph Roswell Hawley (1826–1905) was a Civil War general as well as a politician and newspaper editor. He served as the governor of Connecticut, in the U.S. House of Representatives, and in the U.S. Senate.

56. Simon Cameron (1799–1889) was a U.S. senator and former secretary of war during the Civil War.

57. The name for the place in France where Henry VIII of England and Francis I of France met in 1520 to affirm their friendship following the Anglo-French treaty of 1514.

58. The crest and motto of the Prince of Wales, based on the story of Edward, the Black Prince, and his role in the 1346 Battle of Crécy. The sixteen-year-old Edward, moved by the valor of the sightless King John of Bohemia, who had died in battle, took three ostrich feathers from King John's crest as well as his motto "Ich dein" ("I serve").

59. Counterfeit, sham, not genuine; of the nature of a cheap or showy imitation (from the OED).

60. Matthew Somerville Morgan (1839–1890) was a cartoonist, theater manager, and pioneer of theatrical lithography. He was first hired by artistic director Steele Mackaye to paint scenery for Cody and Salsbury's *The Drama of Civilization,* staged in Madison Square Garden in 1887. The Manchester season reintroduced many elements of the earlier show that had been dropped during London's outdoor season.

61. One after another, one by one in succession (from the OED).

62. A Greek poet from the sixth century BCE, said to be one of the founders of Greek drama.

63. Sir John Richard Somers Vine (1847–1929) was the private secretary to the Lord Mayor and the author of a book on English municipal institutions.

64. Henry Wadsworth Longfellow (1807–1882) was a popular American poet of the mid-nineteenth century. Longfellow was the most commercially successful poet of his generation and his works sold well in both the United States and England. This poem appears to imitate Longfellow's 1855 epic poem *The Song of Hiawatha* with its trochaic tetrameter. The Native American words, such as the Ojibwe "Gichigami" ("Gitche-Gumee" in the poem, meaning "big water" in reference to Lake Superior), as well as "Muskoday," "Ozawa'beek," and "Ke-neu," are direct allusions to the earlier poem.

65. In his 1879 autobiography Cody claims this as a name the Indians used for him, meaning "Long Hair."

66. Jupiter is the Roman god who controls the weather.

67. In the open air.

SELECTED BIBLIOGRAPHY

Black Elk, Nicholas, and John G. Neihardt. *Black Elk Speaks: Being the Life Story of a Holy Man of the Oglala Sioux*. Lincoln: University of Nebraska Press, 2004.

Buffalo Bill. *Story of the Wild West and Camp-Fire Chats by Buffalo Bill*. Philadelphia: Historical Publishing Company, 1888.

Burke, John M. *"Buffalo Bill" from Prairie to Palace: An Authentic History of the Wild West, with Sketches, Stories of Adventure and Anecdotes of "Buffalo Bill," the Hero of the Plains*. Lincoln: University of Nebraska Press, 2012.

Cody, William F. *The Life of Hon. William F. Cody, Known as Buffalo Bill*. Lincoln: University of Nebraska Press, 2011.

Flint, Kate. *The Transatlantic Indian, 1776–1930*. Princeton: Princeton University Press, 2008.

Gallop, Alan. *Buffalo Bill's British Wild West*. Gloucestershire: The History Press, 2009.

Kasson, Joy S. *Buffalo Bill's Wild West: Celebrity, Memory, and Popular History*. New York: Hill and Wang, 2000.

Lamar, Howard R., ed. *The New Encyclopedia of the American West*. New Haven: Yale University Press, 1998.

Milner, Clyde A., II, Carol A. O'Connor, and Martha A. Sandweiss, eds. *The Oxford History of the American West*. New York: Oxford University Press, 1994.

Russell, Don. *The Lives and Legends of Buffalo Bill*. Norman: University of Oklahoma Press, 1979.

Rydell, Robert W. "London's American Exhibition of 1887: How a Cultural Farce Became a Political Force." In *Over (T)here: Transatlantic Essays in Honor of Rob Kroes*, ed. Kate Delaney and Ruud Janssens. Amsterdam: VU University Press, 2005.

Rydell, Robert W., and Rob Kroes. *Buffalo Bill in Bologna: The Americanization of the World, 1869–1922*. Chicago: University of Chicago Press, 2005.

Slotkin, Richard. *Gunfighter Nation: The Myth of the Frontier in Twentieth-Century America*. Norman: University of Oklahoma Press, 1998.

Standing Bear, Luther. *My People the Sioux*. Lincoln: University of Nebraska Press, 2006.

Turner, Frederick Jackson. *Frontier and Section*. Englewood Cliffs NJ: Prentice Hall, 1961.

Warren, Louis S. *Buffalo Bill's America: William Cody and the Wild West Show*. New York: Alfred A. Knopf, 2005.

Wilmeth, Don B., and Christopher Bigsby, eds. *The Cambridge History of American Theater*. 2 Vols. New York: Cambridge University Press, 1998.

INDEX

In the Papers of William F. "Buffalo Bill" Cody series

Four Years in Europe with Buffalo Bill
Charles Eldridge Griffin
Edited and with an introduction by Chris Dixon

The Life of Hon. William F. Cody, Known as Buffalo Bill
William F. Cody
Edited and with an introduction by Frank Christianson

Buffalo Bill from Prairie to Palace
John M. Burke
Edited and with an introduction by Chris Dixon

The Wild West in England
William F. Cody
Edited and with an introduction by Frank Christianson

To order or obtain more information on these
or other University of Nebraska Press titles,
visit www.nebraskapress.unl.edu.